VOGUE KNITTING
SOCKS

VOGUE KNITTING
SOCKS

SIXTH&SPRING BOOKS
NEW YORK

SIXTH&SPRING BOOKS
233 Spring Street
New York, New York 10013

Library of Congress Cataloging-in-Publication Data

Vogue knitting socks / [editor-in-chief, Trisha Malcolm].
  p. cm -- (Vogue knitting on the go!)
Originally published: New York : Butterick, 1998
ISBN 1-931543-17-8
  1. Knitting--Patterns. 2. Socks. I. Title: Socks. II. Malcolm, Trisha, 1960- III. Series.

TT825.V647 2002
746.43'20432--dc21

                                        2002017609

Manufactured in China

1 3 5 7 9 10 8 6 4 2

Second Edition

TABLE OF CONTENTS

INTRODUCTION

With the constant push and pull of today's busy lifestyle, getting everything done takes more than a fair share of juggling. It's hard enough to fit the "must-do's" into our crowded schedules, let alone make time for life's simple pleasures (knitting among them). Take heart! Your day is filled with windows of knitting opportunity. Get clicking on the bus ride to work, in the doctor's waiting room or while you're on hold on the phone. The projects in the *Knitting on the Go* series are designed for just such spare moments. Compact pieces—small in scale, but big in creative outlet—that you can take along with you.

Socks are wonderful on-the-go projects. Small enough to slip into a bag, they are an enticing way to try out new color combinations, stitch patterns and techniques—without a huge investment in time or materials. They make great gifts too!

Express yourself—socks are fun! Each of the designs in this book has a personality all its own—and you probably have just the person in your life to fit every sock! Use the wonderful array of yarns suggested in the patterns or pull from your stash. Let your imagination run wild, just be sure to make a test swatch for gauge. When you like what you see, start stitching!

So set your sights on a sock, grab your needles and get ready to **KNIT ON THE GO...**

THE BASICS

Socks, or "stockings" as some still call them, have been knit for hundreds of years all around the world. In many countries children are taught to knit socks at a young age. To those without the benefit of this experience, sock-knitting may appear sophisticated. Actually, "turning" a heel is an easy skill to master and the excitement of seeing the heel develop adds a certain momentum to sock-knitting. Socks can be constructed in all manners—knit in-the-round on double pointed needles or knit flat and then seamed—and just about any type of patterning can be incorporated into a sock's design. This book explores many variations and sets out the basics, so you can please your feet and the feet of those you love with beautiful socks.

SOCK CONSTRUCTION

Most of the socks in this book have been knit in rounds on a set of 4 or 5 double pointed needles (dpn). This eliminates seams at heels and toes, making them more comfortable for the wearer.

The toes, and heels, are woven together using the Kitchener stitch. The Kitchener stitch mimics a knit stitch, is neat, and provides an invisible seam (see page 15).

The few exceptions to circular sock knitting are the Argyle Socks, Bed Socks and Fair Isle Socks. The Bed Socks are seamed along the instep for easy working; the Argyle socks have a flat-worked instep, and the Fair Isle pattern is worked flat for the sock cuff only.

Cuff

All the socks in this book begin with the cuff. Stitches are cast on to one needle, then divided onto three or four needles to work in rounds. This helps keep the stitches from twisting on the first round. For most socks, the number of stitches on the cuff will equal the number of stitches on the foot after the heel and instep shaping are completed.

Heel

After the cuff is the desired length, stitches are generally divided in half and shifted around the needles so that the center of the heel is the beginning of the cuff rounds. The remaining instep (front of foot) stitches are divided onto two needles to be worked later.

The heel is then worked straight (that is back and forth in rows), until it is the desired depth. The heel is then shaped with short rows into a V-shape or a curved U-shape.

Instep

To begin working in rounds again, as well as to join instep to heel, stitches are knit and repositioned again so that the round begins at the center of the heel (or sole). Stitches are picked up and knit along each side of the heel piece, joining heel and instep. Then the instep is shaped in a wedge shape, sometimes called a gusset, with decreases usually spelled out on the first and third needles only.

Foot

When the heel shaping is complete, the foot is worked straight, resuming original patterns, until the sock foot measures 2"/5cm less than the desired length from the end of the heel to the end of the toe.

Toe

Once again, if the stitches are not already in the correct alignment, they are shifted so that half the stitches are on Needle 2 and the other half of the stitches are divided onto

Needles 1 and 3. Then double decreases are worked at each side edge of the toe to the required length.

SIZING

Sock sizing is as individual as shoe sizing. General sizing information is given with each set of instructions. Styles are categorized as woman's, man's, child's, infant's or adults, with a general length given.

The best approach to fit is to measure the foot of the wearer (from end of heel to end of toe) and knit the foot length accordingly. Individual taste and wearing style also help determine fit, whether it be a house sock, boot sock or dress sock.

YARN SELECTION

For an exact reproduction of the socks photographed, use the yarn listed in the materials section of the pattern. We've chosen yarns that are readily available in the U.S. and Canada at the time of printing. The Resources list on pages 94 and 95 provides addresses of yarn distributors. Contact them for the name of a retailer in your area.

YARN SUBSTITUTION

You may wish to substitute yarns. Perhaps you view small-scale projects as a chance to incorporate leftovers from your yarn stash, or the yarn specified may not be available in your area. You'll need to knit to the given gauge to obtain the knitted measurements with a substitute yarn (see "Gauge" on page 12). Be sure to consider how the fiber content of the substitute yarn will affect the comfort and the ease of care of your socks.

To facilitate yarn substitution, *Vogue Knitting* grades yarn by the standard stitch gauge obtained in Stockinette stitch. You'll find a grading number in the "Materials" section of the pattern, immediately following the fiber type of the yarn. Look for a substitute yarn that falls into the same category. The suggested gauge on the ball band should be comparable to that on the Yarn Symbols chart (below).

After you've successfully gauge-swatched a substitute yarn, you'll need to figure out how much of the substitute yarn the project requires. First, find the total length of the original yarn in the pattern (multiply number of balls by yards/meters per ball). Divide this figure by the new yards/meters per ball (listed on the ball band). Round up to the next whole number. The answer is the number of balls required.

FOLLOWING CHARTS

Charts are a convenient way to follow colorwork, lace, cable and other stitch patterns at a glance. *Vogue Knitting* stitch charts utilize

YARN SYMBOLS

① **Fine Weight**
(29-32 stitches per 4"/10cm)
Includes baby and fingering yarns, and some of the heavier crochet cottons.

② **Lightweight**
(25-28 stitches per 4"/10cm)
Includes sport yarn, sock yarn, UK 4-ply and lightweight DK yarns.

③ **Medium Weight**
(21-24 stitches per 4"/10cm)
Includes DK and worsted, the most commonly used knitting yarns.

④ **Medium-heavy Weight**
(17-20 stitches per 4"/10cm)
Also called heavy worsted or Aran.

⑤ **Bulky Weight**
(13-16 stitches per 4"/10cm)
Also called chunky. Includes heavier Icelandic yarns.

⑥ **Extra-bulky Weight**
(9-12 stitches per 4"/10cm)
The heaviest yarns available.

GAUGE

It is always important to knit a gauge swatch, and it is even more so with socks as they are designed to fit the foot. If your gauge is too loose, you could end up with sloppy slipper-socks instead of anklets; if it's too tight, you could end up with a sock that has to be pulled over the heel using a shoehorn.

Making a flat gauge swatch for socks knit in the round will allow you to measure gauge over a 4"/10cm span that will lay flat for better reading. However, when a sock includes a complex stitch pattern knit in rounds, a circularly-knit swatch will test the gauge best and the practice will familiarize you with the pattern—cast on at least as many stitches required for the sock. The type of needles used—straight or double pointed, wood or metal—will influence gauge, so knit your swatch with the needles you plan to use for the project. Measure gauge as illustrated. Try different needle sizes until your sample measures the required number of stitches and rows. To get fewer stitches to the inch/cm, use larger needles; to get more stitches to the inch/cm, use smaller needles.

Knitting in the round may tighten the gauge, so if you measured the gauge on a flat swatch, take another gauge reading after you begin your sock. When the sock measures at least 2"/5cm after the cuff, lay it flat and measure over the stitches in the center of the piece, as the side stitches may be distorted. Keep in mind that if you consciously try to loosen your tension to match the flat knit swatch you can prevent having to go up a needle size.

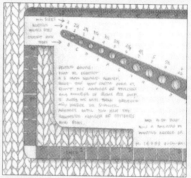

the universal knitting language of "symbolcraft." When knitting in the round, read charts from right to left on every round, repeating any stitch and row repeats as directed in the pattern. When knitting back and forth in rows, read charts from right to left on right side (RS) rows and from left to right on wrong side (WS) rows. Posting a self-adhesive note under your working row is an easy way to keep track of your place on a chart.

COLORWORK KNITTING

Two main types of colorwork are explored in this book.

Intarsia

Intarsia is accomplished with separate bobbins of individual colors. This method is ideal for large blocks of color or for motifs that aren't repeated close together, such as the Argyle Socks. When changing colors, always pick up the new color and wrap it around the old color to prevent holes.

For smaller areas of color, such as the cross lines on Argyle diamonds, duplicate stitch embroidery works best after the pieces are knit (see page 15).

Stranding

When motifs are closely placed, colorwork

is accomplished by stranding along two or more colors per row, creating "floats" on the wrong side of the fabric. This technique is sometimes called Fair Isle knitting after the traditional Fair Isle patterns composed of small motifs with frequent color changes.

To keep an even tension and prevent holes while knitting, pick up yarns alternately over and under one another across or around. While knitting, stretch the stitches on the needle slightly wider than the length of the float at the back to keep work from puckering.

When changing colors at the beginning of rows or rounds, carry yarn along for a few rows only, or cut yarn and rejoin when needed. It is important to keep the "floats" small and neat so that toes don't catch on them when pulling on socks.

LACE
Lace knitting provides a feminine touch to some of the socks featured in this book. Knitted lace is formed with "yarn overs," which create an eyelet hole, in combination with decreases that create directional effects. To make a yarn over (yo), merely pass the yarn over the right-hand needle to form a new loop. Decreases are worked as k2tog, SSK or SKP depending on the desired slant and are spelled out specifically with each instruction. On the row or round that follows the lace or eyelet detail, each yarn over is treated as one stitch. If you're new to lace knitting, it's a good idea to count the stitches at the end of each row or round. Making a gauge swatch in the stitch pattern enables you to practice a new lace pattern. Instead of binding off the swatch, place the final row on a holder, as the bind off tends to pull in the stitches and distort the gauge.

BLOCKING
Blocking is an all-important finishing step in the knitting process. Most sock styles will retain their best shape by pressing flat with a slight fold line down the center of the instep and heel. When working flat insteps or cuffs in rows instead of rounds (such as the Argyles or Fair Isle socks), pin and block flat areas first before joining.

Wet Block Method
Pin pieces to measurements on a flat surface and lightly dampen using a spray bottle. Allow to dry before removing pins.

Steam Block Method
Pin pieces to measurements or smooth into place with hands. Steam lightly, holding the iron approximately 2"/5cm above the knitting. Do not press an iron onto any knitting, as it will flatten the stitches.

CARE
Hand-knit socks require the same care as hand-knit sweaters. Hand wash one pair of socks at a time for best results. Use cold water and dissolve soap flakes or a mild detergent before immersing the socks. Let socks soak for 5-10 minutes, then gently squeeze suds through, never pulling or rubbing. Rinse with plenty of water until all soap is washed away. Gently squeeze out water then blot between layers of towels to absorb any excess. Lay flat to dry, pressing to original measurements with hands.

FINISHING TECHNIQUES
The socks in this book make use of embroidered, knitted and crocheted embellishments as well as trims made with yarn. Embroidery stitches are illustrated in specific patterns, as needed. Directions for making pom-poms can be found on page 14—use them at the heel of a classic tennis footlet, or add a few to the sock of your choice. You'll also want to refer to illustrations at the end of this section for other useful techniques: double cast on becomes a two-colored edge on the Yoruba socks; crochet stitches lend a fanciful touch to the Turkish socks; and Kitchener stitch makes a seamless toe for every sock.

POM-POM TEMPLATE

POM-POM

I Following the template, cut two circular pieces of cardboard.

2 Hold the two circles together and wrap the yarn tightly around the cardboard several times. Secure and carefully cut the yarn.

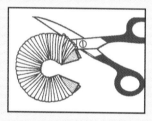

3 Tie a piece a yarn tightly between the two circles. Remove the cardboard and trim the pom-pom to the desired size.

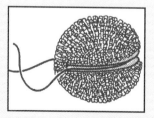

DOUBLE CAST ON

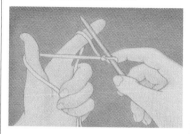

I *Make a slip knot on the right needle, leaving a long tail. Wind the tail end around your left thumb, front to back. Wrap the yarn from the ball over your left index finger and secure the ends in your palm.*

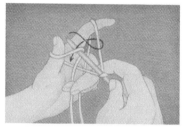

2 *Insert the needle upwards in the loop on your thumb. Then with the needle, draw the yarn from the ball through the loop to form a stitch.*

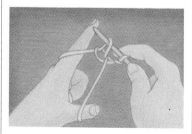

3 *Take your thumb out of the loop and tighten the loop on the needle. Continue in this way until all the stitches are cast on.*

THE KITCHENER STITCH

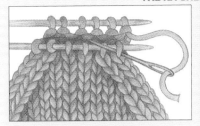

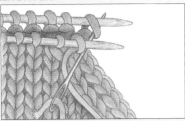

I *Insert tapestry needle purlwise (as shown) through first stitch on front needle. Pull yarn through, leaving that stitch on knitting needle.*

2 *Insert tapestry needle knitwise (as shown) through first stitch on back needle. Pull yarn through, leaving stitch on knitting needle.*

3 *Insert tapestry needle knitwise through first stitch on front needle, slip stitch off needle and insert tapestry needle purlwise (as shown) through next stitch on front needle. Pull yarn through, leaving this stitch on needle.*

4 *Insert tapestry needle purlwise through first stitch on back needle. Slip stitch off needle and insert tapestry needle knitwise (as shown) through next stitch on back needle. Pull yarn through, leaving this stitch on needle.*
Repeat steps 3 and 4 until all stitches on both front and back needles have been grafted. Fasten off and weave in end.

DUPLICATE STITCH

Duplicate stitch covers a knit stitch. Bring the needle up below the stitch to be worked. Insert the needle under both loops one row above and pull it through. Insert it back into the stitch below and through the center of the next stitch in one motion, as shown.

CROCHET STITCHES

CHAIN

1 *Pass the yarn over the hook and catch it with the hook.*

2 *Draw the yarn through the loop on the hook.*

3 *Repeat steps 1 and 2 to make a chain.*

SINGLE CROCHET

1 *Insert the hook through top two loops of a stitch. Pass the yarn over the hook and draw up a loop—two loops on hook.*

2 *Pass the yarn over the hook and draw through both loops on hook.*

3 *Continue in the same way, inserting the hook into each stitch.*

HALF-DOUBLE CROCHET

1 *Pass the yarn over the hook. Insert the hook through the top two loops of a stitch.*

2 *Pass the yarn over the hook and draw up a loop—three loops on hook. Pass the yarn over the hook.*

3 *Draw through all three loops on hook.*

DOUBLE CROCHET

1 *Pass the yarn over the hook. Insert the hook through the top two loops of a stitch.*

2 *Pass the yarn over the hook and draw up a loop— three loops on hook.*

SLIP STITCH

Insert the crochet hook into a stitch, catch the yarn and pull up a loop. Draw the loop through the loop on the hook.

3 *Pass the yarn over the hook and draw it through the first two loops on the hook, pass the yarn over the hook and draw through the remaining two loops. Continue in the same way, inserting the hook into each stitch.*

KNITTING TERMS AND ABBREVIATIONS

approx approximately

beg begin(ning)

bind off Used to finish an edge and keep stitches from unraveling. Lift the first stitch over the second, the second over the third, etc. (UK: cast off)

cast on A foundation row of stitches placed on the needle in order to begin knitting.

CC contrast color

ch chain(s)

cm centimeter(s)

cont continu(e)(ing)

dc double crochet (UK: tr-treble)

dec decrease(ing)—Reduce the stitches in a row (knit 2 together).

dpn double pointed needle(s)

foll follow(s)(ing)

g gram(s)

garter stitch Knit every row. Circular knitting: knit one round, then purl one round.

hdc half-double crochet (UK: htr-half treble)

inc increase(ing)—Add stitches in a row (knit into the front and back of a stitch).

k knit

k2tog knit 2 stitches together

lp(s) loops(s)

LH left-hand

m meter(s)

M1 make one stitch—With the needle tip, lift the strand between last stitch worked and next stitch on the left-hand needle and knit into the back of it. One stitch has been added.

MC main color

mm millimeter(s)

no stitch On some charts, "no stitch" is indicated with shaded spaces where stitches have been decreased or not yet made. In such cases, work the stitches of the chart, skipping over the "no stitch" spaces.

oz ounce(s)

p purl

p2tog purl 2 stitches together

pat pattern

pick up and knit (purl) Knit (or purl) into the loops along an edge.

pm place markers—Place or attach a loop of contrast yarn or purchased stitch marker as indicated.

rem remain(s)(ing)

rep repeat

rev St st reverse Stockinette stitch—Purl right-side rows, knit wrong-side rows. Circular knitting: purl all rounds. (UK: reverse stocking stitch)

rnd(s) round(s)

RH right-hand

RS right side(s)

sc single crochet (UK: dc - double crochet)

sk skip

SKP Slip 1, knit 1, pass slip stitch over knit 1.

sl slip—An unworked stitch made by passing a stitch from the left-hand to the right-hand needle as if to purl.

sl st slip stitch (UK: single crochet)

SSK slip, slip, knit— Slip next 2 stitches knitwise, one at a time, to right-hand needle. Insert tip of left-hand needle into fronts of these stitches from left to right. Knit them together. One stitch has been decreased.

st(s) stitch(es)

St st Stockinette stitch—Knit right-side rows, purl wrong-side rows. Circular knitting: knit all rounds. (UK: stocking stitch)

tbl through back of loop

tog together

WS wrong side(s)

wyif with yarn in front

wyib with yarn in back

work even Continue in pattern without increasing or decreasing. (UK: work straight)

yd yard(s)

yo yarn over—Make a new stitch by wrapping the yarn over the right-hand needle. (UK: yfwd, yon, yrn)

* Repeat directions following * as many times as indicated.

[ ] Repeat directions inside brackets as many times as indicated.

Elaborately-detailed socks, designed by Mari Lynn Patrick, feature the Turkish stocking symbols "baklava slice" and "cengel" (hook). The cengel symbol dates back to a 5th century B.C. felt stocking excavated at Pazyryk.

SIZES

Instructions are written for woman's size Large or man's Small.

MATERIALS

■ 2 1¾oz/50g balls (each approx 138yd/128m) of Filatura di Crosa/Stacy Charles *501* (wool③) in #115 black (A)
■ 1 ball each in #2151 rust (B), #106 white (C), #185 lime (D), #210 blue (E), #2113 teal (F), #2119 purple (G), #204 tan (H), #453 ochre (I), #214 olive (J)
■ 1 set (4) size 3 (3mm) double pointed needles (dpn) OR SIZE TO OBTAIN GAUGE
■ Size 1 (2mm) steel crochet hook
■ Stitch markers
■ Tapestry needle

GAUGE

25 sts and 28 rnds to 4"/10cm over St st and chart pat using size 3 (3mm) needles. TAKE TIME TO CHECK GAUGE.

Note When changing colors, twist yarns on WS to prevent holes.

CUFF

Note Sts 1-5 on chart form 5-st spiral pat for side panel.

Beg at top edge with B, on one needle cast on 60 sts. Divide sts on three needles as foll: 22 sts on *Needle 1*; 16 sts on *Needle 2*; 22 sts on *Needle 3*. Join, taking care not to twist sts on needles. Mark end of rnd and sl marker every rnd. Beg working pat foll chart rnd 1 (work 30-st rep twice) as foll: sts 1-22 on *Needle 1*; sts 23-30 then sts 1-8 on *Needle 2*; sts 9-30 on *Needle 3*. Cont to foll chart in this way through rnd 49.

HEEL

K3, then sl these 3 sts to end of *Needle 3*. K next 30 sts onto *Needle 1*, working chart row 20, for heel. Divide rem 30 sts onto two needles to be worked later for instep.

Note For heel sts only, omit 5-st spiral pat (sts 1-5 on chart) and cont these 5 sts in chart pat as established.

Cont to work back and forth on heel sts in St st and chart foll rows 20-34 for heel. Heel measures approx 2"/5cm.

Turn heel

Working chart rows 11 and 12 only (colors C and A), turn heel as foll:

Next row (RS) K17 (half the number of heel sts plus 2), k2tog, k1, turn.

Row 2 Sl 1, p5, p2tog, p1, turn.

Row 3 Sl 1, k6, k2tog, k1, turn.

Row 4 Sl 1, p7, p2tog, p1, turn.

Cont in this way always having 1 more st before dec, and work k2tog on RS rows or p2tog on WS rows, until there are 18 sts on heel needle.

Note While working instep, resume chart pat rows 20-34. Then turn chart upside down and working in reverse, work rows 19-4.

Shape instep

Next rnd Foll rnd 20 of chart, k9 and leave on needle; with spare needle, k9 (the rem sts of heel) then pick up and k 16 sts along side of heel piece; with *Needle 2* work across 30 instep sts; with *Needle 3* pick up and k 16 sts along other side of heel piece, k9 from *Needle 1*—80 sts. Divide sts so that there are 24 sts on *Needle 1*; 33 sts on *Needle 2* (instep); and 23 sts on *Needle 3*. Resume 5-st spiral pat in A, B and C (sts 1-5 on chart) and work as foll:

Rnd 1 Knit.

Rnd 2 *Needle 1* k to last 2 sts, k2tog; *Needle 2* knit; Needle 3 SKP, k to end of needle.

Rep these 2 rnds until there are 60 sts on all three needles. Then cont in pat, working chart rnds 19-4, then work rnds 20-34 ONLY until sock measures 8"/20.5cm or 2"/5cm less than desired length from back of heel to end of toe. (Make adjustments in length at this point.)

Shape toe

Note Work chart rnds 11 and 12 only (colors C and A) while shaping toe.

Beg at center of sole, place 60 sts on three needles as foll: 15 sts on *Needle 1*; 30 sts on *Needle 2*; 15 sts on *Needle 3*. Place marker for end of rnd and join to work in rnds.

Rnd 1 *Needle 1* k to last 3 sts, k2tog, k1; *Needle 2* k1, SKP, k to last 3 sts, k2tog, k1; *Needle 3* k1, SKP, k to end.

Rnd 2 Knit.

Rep these 2 rnds until there are 8 sts on *Needle 2*. Place sts from *Needle 1* and *Needle 3* on same needle. Weave sts tog using Kitchener stitch.

FINISHING

Block socks. With crochet hook and J, working from WS around cuff edge of sock, work 1 sc into each A lp under B cast-on edge at top (cast-on edge will form a ridge on RS). Join and turn to work edge from RS.

Next rnd Ch 3, *1 dc and 1 hdc in first sc, sl st in next sc; rep from * around.
Fasten off.

Color key

Black (A)

Rust (B)

White (C)

Lime (D)

Blue (E)

Teal (F)

Purple (G)

Tan (H)

Ochre (I)

Olive (J)

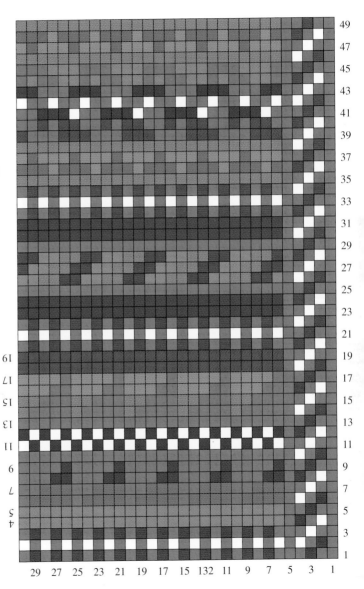

LEAF SOCKS
Falling leaves over autumnal stripes

For Intermediate Knitters

Tweedy, striped socks embroidered with tumbling leaves, designed by Gitta Schrade. Knit one in each color way, or match colors for a double set.

SIZES

Instructions are for woman's size Medium. Changes for size Large are in parentheses.

MATERIALS

Dark Green Socks

- 1 1¾oz/50g ball (each approx 226yd/205m) of Stahl Wolle/Tahki Imports *Socka 50* (wool/polyamide①) in #9458 dark green (A), #9423 light olive (B), #9424 cinnamon (C), and #9437 burgundy (D)

Burgundy Socks

- 1 1¾oz/50g ball (each approx 226yd/205m) of Stahl Wolle/Tahki Imports *Socka 50* (wool/polyamide①) in #9437 burgundy (A), #9423 light olive (B), #9424 cinnamon (C), and #9459 jade (D)

Both versions

- 1 1¾oz/50g ball (each approx 226yd/205m) of Stahl Wolle/Tahki Imports *Socka Color* (wool/polyamide①) in #9139 multi (MC)
- 1 set (5) each sizes 1 and 2 (2.25 and 2.5mm) double pointed needles (dpn) OR SIZE TO OBTAIN GAUGE
- Stitch markers
- Tapestry needle

GAUGE

32 sts and 42 rnds to 4"/10cm over St st using larger needles. TAKE TIME TO CHECK GAUGE.

STITCHES USED

Stripe Pattern

K3 rnds MC, 3 rnds A, 4 rnds MC, 13 rnds A, 3 rnds MC, 5 rnds A, 3 rnds MC, 3 rnds A, 6 rnds MC, 4 rnds A (47 rnds). Work striped pat to toe.

CUFF

Beg at top edge with smaller needles and MC, cast on 60 (68) sts on one needle. Divide sts on three needles as foll: 22 (25) sts on *Needle 1*; 16 (18) sts on *Needle 2*; 22 (25) sts on *Needle 3*. Join, taking care not to twist sts on needles. Mark end of rnd and sl marker every rnd. Work in St st (k every rnd) for 4 rnds. Then, work in k1, p1 rib for 12 rnds. Change to larger needles and work 47 rnds of stripe pat.

HEEL

With spare needle, k15 (17) sts from *Needle 1*, then sl 15 (17) sts from *Needle 3* onto other end of spare needle—30 (34) sts for heel on spare needle. Divide rem 30 (34) sts onto *Needle 2* and *Needle 3* to be worked later for instep. Work back and forth in rows on heel sts only.

Row I (WS) With MC, sl 1, p to end.
Row 2 With MC, sl 1, k to end.
Rep these 2 rows for a total of 22 (26) heel rows.

Turn heel

Cont to work heel with MC only.

Next row (RS) K20 (23) sts, SSK, turn.

Row 2 Sl 1, p10 (12), p2tog, turn.

Row 3 Sl 1, k10 (12), SSK, turn.

Rep last 2 rows until all sts are worked—12 (14) on heel needle.

Next rnd (RS) K6 (7) sts and leave on needle. With spare needle, k6 (7) sts, (the rem sts of heel), with same needle pick up and k 15 (17) sts along side of heel piece, pm; with *Needle 2* k30 (34) sts from instep, pm; with *Needle 3* pick up and k 15 (17) sts along other side of heel piece, k rem 6 (7) sts of heel—72 (82) sts.

Shape instep

Rnd 1 K to 2 sts before marker, k2tog, k to 2nd marker, SSK, k to end of rnd.

Work 2 rnds even. Rep last 3 rnds until there are 60 (68) sts. Work even in stripe pat until foot measures 6¾ (7¾)"/17 (19.5)cm or 2¼"/5.75cm less than desired length from back of heel to end of toe.

Shape toe

Cont to work toe shaping with MC only. Divide sts onto 3 needles as foll: 15 (17) sts on *Needle 1*; 30 (34) sts on *Needle 2*; 15 (17) sts on *Needle 3*.

Dec rnd *Needle 1* k to last 3 sts, k2tog, k1; *Needle 2* k1, SSK, k to last 3 sts, k2tog, k1; *Needle 3* k1, SSK, k to end. Work 3 rnds even. [Work dec rnd, work 2 rnds even] twice. [Work dec rnd, work 1 rnd even] 3 times. Then work dec rnd every rnd until 8 sts rem. Place sts on two needles and weave tog using Kitchener stitch.

FINISHING

Block socks. With double strand of yarn embroider leaves foll chart and photo for colors, with stem stitch inside and satin stitch outside. Foll photo and diagram, work leaves 1 and 2 at top of sock, leaf 3 at top of heel and leaves 4 and 5 on other side of sock.

EMBROIDERY STITCHES

Stem Stitch

Bring needle up on edge of area to be outlined. Insert it a short distance to the right at an angle and pull it through, emerging at the midpoint of the previous stitch. Work left to right, keeping the thread below the needle.

Satin Stitch

Bring needle up at one side of space to be covered and take a straight stitch to the other side. Repeat this step, bringing needle up next to the previous stitch, completely filling the space. Take care not to pull stitches tightly to avoid puckering.

DARK GREEN SOCKS
EMBROIDERY DIAGRAM

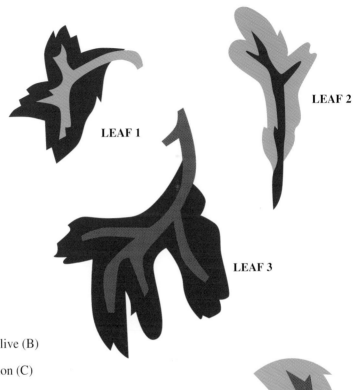

LEAF 1

LEAF 2

LEAF 3

Color key

- Light Olive (B)
- Cinnamon (C)
- Burgundy (D)

LEAF 4

LEAF 5

Note For Burgundy
Socks, substitute
Jade for Burgundy

LEALT SOCKS

Lace from the Scottish Isles

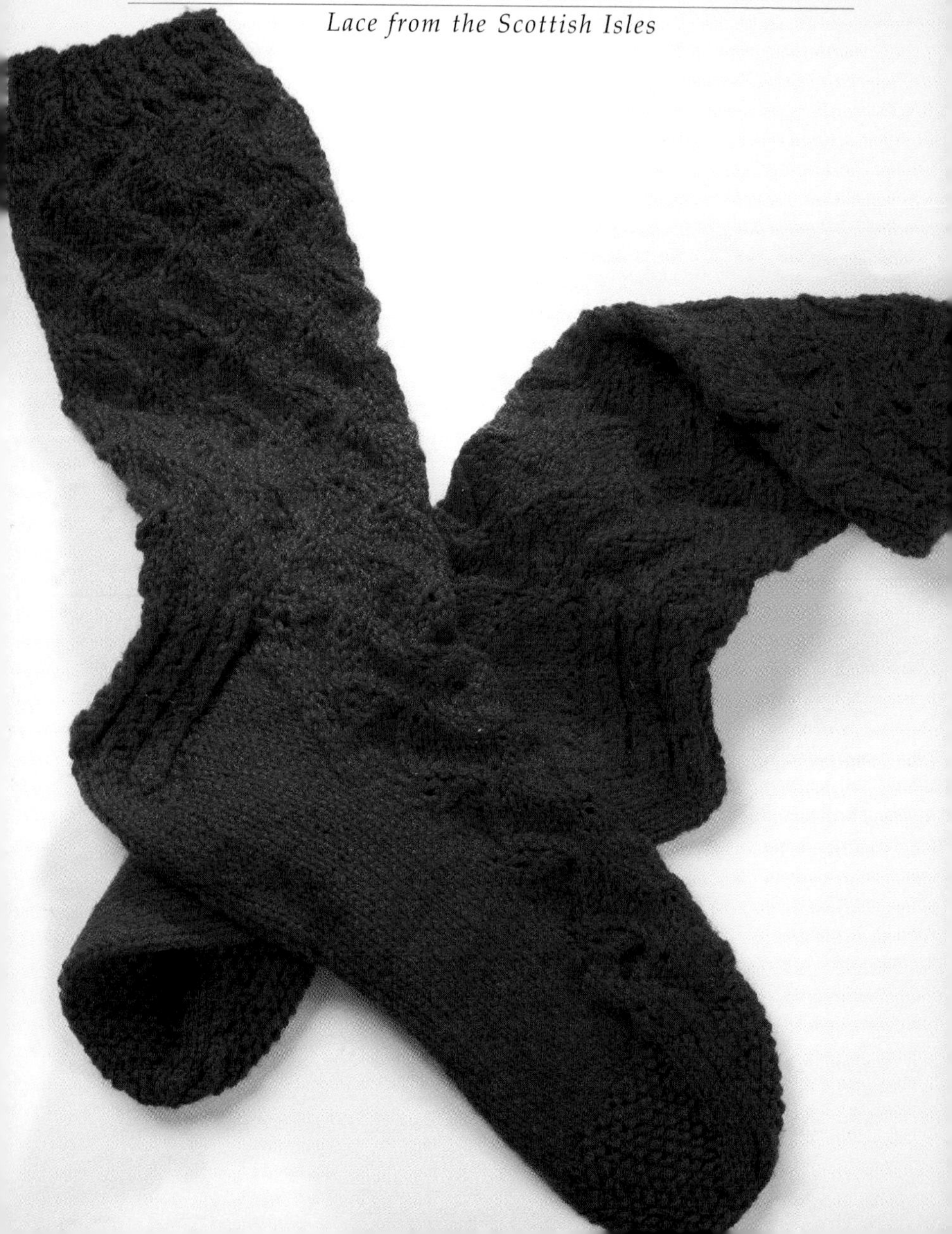

Named after a much-loved family home on the Scotttish Isle of Jura, these socks, designed by Jean Moss, take inspiration from the traditional lace knitting techniques of the region.

SIZE
Instructions are written for woman's size Large.

MATERIALS
- 2 1¾oz/50g balls (each approx 184yd/170m) of Rowan *4-Ply Botany* (wool①) in #550 sorrel
- 1 set (4) size 3 (3mm) double pointed needles (dpn) OR SIZE TO OBTAIN GAUGE

GAUGE
28 sts and 38 rnds to 4"/10cm over lace pat using size 3 (3mm) needles. TAKE TIME TO CHECK GAUGE.

Note Double cast-on method is used for cast-on edge of cuff (see Basics section for technique). Another method of casting on, however, may be used.

STITCHES USED
Lacy Rib (in the round) multiple of 5 sts
Rnds I and 3 (RS) *P2, k3; rep from * around.
Rnd 2 *P2, k2tog, yo, k1; rep from * around.
Rnd 4 *P2, k1, yo, SSK; rep from * around.
Rep these 4 rnds for lacy rib.

Lacy Rib for heel multiple of 5 sts plus 2
Rows I and 3 (WS) K2, *p3, k2; rep from * to end.
Row 2 P2, *k1, yo, SSK, p2; rep from * to end.
Row 4 P2, *k2tog, yo, k1, p2; rep from * to end.
Rep these 4 rows for lacy rib for heel.

Lace Pattern (multiple of 8 sts)
Rnd I (RS) *Yo, k1 tbl, yo, SKP, k5; rep from * around.
Rnd 2 *K3, SKP, k4; rep from * around.
Rnd 3 *Yo, k1 tbl, yo, k2, SKP, k3; rep from * around.
Rnd 4 *K5, SKP, k2; rep from * around.
Rnd 5 *K1 tbl, yo, k4, SKP, k1, yo; rep from * around.
Rnd 6 *K6, SKP, k1; rep from * around.
Rnd 7 *K5, k2tog, yo, kl tbl, yo; rep from * around.
Rnd 8 *K4, k2tog, k3; rep from * around.
Rnd 9 *K3, k2tog, k2, yo, k1 tbl, yo; rep from * around.
Rnd 10 *K2, k2tog, k5; rep from * around.
Rnd 11 *Yo, k1, k2tog, k4, yo, k1 tbl; rep from * around.
Rnd 12 *K1, k2tog, k6; rep from * around.
Rep these 12 rnds for lace pat.

Seed st (in the round)
Rnd I *K1, p1; rep from * around.
Rnd 2 K the purl and p the knit sts.
Rep rnd 2 for seed st.

CUFF

Cast on 60 sts on one needle using the double cast-on method. Divide sts evenly onto three needles. Join, taking care not to twist sts on needles. Mark end of rnd and sl marker every rnd. Work in lacy rib for 12 rnds, inc 4 sts evenly across last rnd—64 sts. Adjust the sts so that there are 16 sts on *Needle 1*; 32 sts on *Needle 2*; and 16 sts on *Needle 3* (beg of rnd is the back seam line). Work even in lace pat on 64 sts for a total of 60 rnds. Piece measures approx 7½"/19cm from beg.

HEEL

With *Needle 3* k across the 16 sts of *Needle 1*, inc 1 st in each of last 2 sts—34 heel sts. Divide the rem 32 sts onto two needles to be worked later for instep. Cont to work on 34 heel sts only, working back and forth in rows as foll:

Row 1 (WS) K1 tbl, work row 1 of lacy rib for heel to last st, sl last st wyif. Cont in this way (working first and last sts as on row 1) working in lacy rib for heel for a total of 21 rows, dec 1 st on final row (just before sl st)—33 heel sts.

Turn heel

Next row (RS) K1 tbl, k16, k2tog tbl, k1, turn.

Row 2 Sl 1 purlwise, p2, p2tog, p1, turn.

Row 3 Sl 1 purlwise, k to within 1 st of the turning gap, k2tog tbl, k1, turn.

Row 4 Sl 1 purlwise, p to within 1 st of the turning gap, p2tog, p1, turn.

Rep last 2 rows until all sts are worked—17 sts, end with a WS row.

INSTEP

Gusset

Next rnd *Needle 1* sl 1 purlwise, k16 heel sts, pick up and k 16 sts along side of heel piece; with *Needle 2* pick up and k 1 st at beg of instep sts, work across instep sts in established pat (rnd 1 of lace pat), pick up and k 1 st tbl at end of instep sts—34 sts on *Needle 2*; with *Needle 3* pick up and k 16 sts on other side of heel piece, then k first 9 sts from heel needle onto *Needle 3*. There are 24 sts on *Needle 1*; 34 instep sts on *Needle 2*; and 25 sts on *Needle 3*—83 sts in total.

Shape gusset

Rnd 1 (Beg at center back heel) *Needle 1* k to last 3 sts, k2tog, k1; *Needle 2* p2tog then work instep sts in lace pat to last 2 sts, p2tog; *Needle 3* k1, SSK, k to end.

Rnd 2 Work even in St st on *Needle 1* and *Needle 3*, and lace pat (instep sts) on 32 sts of *Needle 2*.

Rnd 3 *Needle 1* k to last 3 sts, k2tog, k1; *Needle 2* work even in lace pat; *Needle 3* k1, SSK, k to end.

Rep last 2 rnds 5 times more, then rep rnd 3 twice—63 sts rem. There are 15 sts on *Needle 1*; 32 sts on *Needle 2*; and 16 sts on *Needle 3*. Cont in pats as established (working lace pat on instep sts only) until sock measures 7½"/19cm or 2"/5cm less than desired length from back of heel to end of toe. (Make adjustments in length at this point.)

Shape toe

Rnd I *Needle 1* work seed st to last 3 sts, k2tog, k1; *Needle 2* k1, SSK, work seed st to last 3 sts, k2tog, k1; *Needle 3* k1, SSK, work seed st to end.

Rnd 2 *Needle 1* work seed st to last 2 sts, k2; *Needle 2* k2, work seed st to last 2 sts, k2; *Needle 3* k2, work seed st to end.

Rep these 2 rnds until 27 sts rem. Then, rep rnd 1 (dec rnd) every rnd until 7 sts rem. Cut yarn leaving end for sewing. Draw through rem 7 sts and pull up to fasten off. Secure and fasten off.

FINISHING

Block socks. Weave in ends neatly.

HIKING SOCKS

Hit the trail

A combination of traditional Anatolian motifs worked in shades of grey, designed by Nadia Severns. Extra heel cushioning and hiking-boot length make these perfect for weekend treks.

SIZE

Instructions are written for woman's size Large.

MATERIALS

■ 1 1¾oz/50g skein (each approx 107yd/98m) of Lion Brand *AL·PA·KA* (acrylic/alpaca/wool/⑤) each in #153 black (A), #152 oxford grey (B), #194 silver grey (C) and #098 natural (D)
■ Small amount of lightweight reinforcing yarn in black (optional)
■ 1 set (4) each sizes 4 and 5 (3.5 and 3.75mm) double pointed needles (dpn) OR SIZE TO OBTAIN GAUGE
■ Stitch markers
■ Tapestry needle

GAUGE

22 sts and 24 rows to 4"/10cm over St st and chart pat using larger needles. TAKE TIME TO CHECK GAUGE.

STITCHES USED

Cable and Garter Rib (multiple of 8 sts)
Rnd 1 K1, k into back of 2nd st, then k into first st, then let both sts fall from needle (C2B), *p3, sl 2 wyib, k1, C2B; rep from *, end last rep sl 2.

Rnd 2 K1, sl 2 wyib, *p3, k into front of 2nd st, then k into first st, then let both sts fall from needle (C2F), k1, sl 2; rep from *, end last rep C2F.
Rnds 3 and 4 Knit.
Rep rnds 1-4 for cable and garter rib.

CUFF

Beg at top edge with A and one smaller needle, cast on 44 sts. Divide sts on smaller needles as foll: 16 sts on *Needle 1*; 14 sts on *Needle 2*; 14 sts on *Needle 3*. Join, taking care not to twist sts on needles. Mark end of rnd and sl marker every rnd. Work in k2, p2 rib for 8 rnds.
Next rnd *Needle 1* k1, inc 1 st, k to last 2 sts, inc 1 st, k1; *Needle 2* k to last 2 sts, inc 1 st, k1; *Needle 3* k to last 2 sts, inc 1 st, k1—48 sts.
Change to larger needles.
Beg chart 1: Rnd 1 Work 12-st rep 4 times.
Cont to foll chart 1 through rnd 12. Change to smaller needles and with B, k 2 rnds. Then cont with B only, redistribute sts so that there are 16 sts on each of the three needles and work 20 rnds (5 reps) of cable and garter rib. Change to larger needles and foll chart 2, working 12-st rep 4 times. Cont to foll chart 2 through rnd 8. Change to smaller needles and with A, k 1 rnd. Cut yarn. Sock measures approx 6½"/16.5cm from beg.
Note If desired, add 1 strand of lightweight yarn to heel and toe sts while knitting to reinforce.

HEEL

Sl last 4 sts from *Needle 3* to end of *Needle 1*, then sl next 5 sts of *Needle 2* to beg of *Needle 1*—25 heel sts. Divide rem 23 sts onto *Needle 2* and *Needle 3* for instep to be worked later. Rejoin A from RS to beg of heel needle.

Next row (RS) K1 tbl, k23, sl 1 wyif.

Row 2 K1 tbl, p23, sl 1 wyif.

Row 3 K1 tbl, *k1, sl 1 purlwise wyib; rep from *, end k1, sl 1 wyif.

Rep last 2 rows for heel for 19 more rows—heel measures approx 2¼"/5.75cm.

Turn heel

Row 1 K16, SSK, turn.

Row 2 Sl 1, p7, p2tog, turn.

Row 3 [Sl 1, k1] 4 times, SSK, turn.

Rep last 2 rows until all heel sts are worked and 9 heel sts rem, end with a WS row. (Cut reinforcing yarn, if necessary.)

Shape gusset

Note To pick up sts along side of heel pieces, use a spare dpn to pick up each edge st without working it, then k1 into back lps of each picked up st when working around.

Rnd 1 With smaller needles and A, [sl 1, k1] 4 times, k1, then with same needle (*Needle 1*), pick up and work into back lps of 13 sts along heel edge; *Needle 2* pick up 1 st tbl at instep, k across 23 instep sts, pick up 1 st tbl at instep; *Needle 3* pick up and work into back lps of 13 sts along heel edge, then k first 4 sts of heel from *Needle 1*. There are 18 sts on *Needle 1*; 25 instep sts on *Needle 2*; and 17 sts on *Needle 3*—60 sts in total.

Rnd 2 With A, work as foll: *Needle 1* k to last 3 sts, k2tog, k1; *Needle 2* SSK, k to last 2 sts, k2tog; *Needle 3* k1, SSK, k to end.

Rnd 3 With B, knit.

Rnd 4 With B, *Needle 1* k to last 3 sts, k2tog, k1; *Needle 2* knit; *Needle 3* k1, SSK, k to end.

Rep last 2 rnds 3 times more working 2 rnds with C, 2 rnds with D and 2 rnds with C—48 sts. There are 13 (sole) sts on *Needle 1*; 23 (instep) sts on *Needle 2*; and 12 (sole) sts on *Needle 3*. Change to larger needles and k 1 rnd with B.

FOOT

Note The 23 sts on *Needle 2* (instep) will be worked foll chart 3 for instep. The 25 sts on *Needle 1* and *Needle 3* (sole) will be worked foll chart 4 for sole.

Rnd 1 *Needle 1* beg with st 1, work sts 1-4 of chart 4 three times, end with st 5; *Needle 2* work sts 1-23 of chart 3; *Needle 3* beg with st 1, work sts 1-4 of chart 4 three times.

Cont to work in this way through rnd 29 of chart 3. Foot measures 8"/20.5cm or 2"/5cm less than desired length from back of heel to end of toe. (Work fewer rows of chart 3 for shorter sock. Return to rnd 1 and work more rnds of chart 3 for longer sock.)

Shape toe

Divide sts so there are 12 sts each on *Needle 1* and *Needle 3* and 24 sts on *Needle 2*.

Rnd 1 With B, k 1 rnd. Rem of toe is worked with A only (and reinforcing yarn if desired).

Rnd 2 With A, work as foll: *Needle 1* k to last 3 sts, k2tog, k1; *Needle 2* k1, SSK, k to last 3 sts, k2tog, k1; *Needle 3* k1, SSK, k to end.

Rnd 3 Knit.

Rep last 2 rnds until 28 sts rem. Then rep rnd 2 (dec rnd) every rnd until 16 sts rem. Place 16 sts on two needles and weave tog using Kitchener stitch.

FINISHING

Block socks, being careful not to flatten rib. Weave in ends neatly.

Color key

 Black (A)

Oxford Grey (B)

Silver Grey (C)

☐ Natural (D)

CHART 2

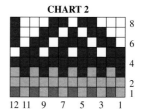

8
6
4
2
1

12 11 9 7 5 3 1

CHART 1

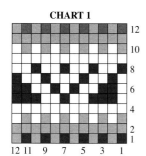

12
10
8
6
4
2
1

12 11 9 7 5 3 1

CHART 3

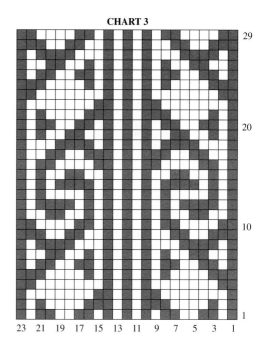

29

20

10

1

23 21 19 17 15 13 11 9 7 5 3 1

CHART 4

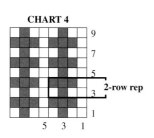

9

7

5

3

1

5 3 1

2-row rep

ARGYLE SOCKS

A boardroom basic

For Intermediate Knitters

Classic argyles, a 50's wardrobe staple, continue to hold their own today. Designed by Jacquelyn Smyth, in re-vamped coloring for strong good looks.

Notes 1 Cast on and work sock back and forth in rows on two needles to toe. Then join and work in rnds while shaping toe. **2** Cross lines may be embroidered in duplicate stitch after socks are knit.

SIZES

Instructions are written for man's size Medium (10½-11½).

MATERIALS

■ 2 1¾oz/50g balls (each approx 184yd/170m) of GGH/Muench *Merino Soft* (wool②) in #29 navy (A)
■ 1 ball each in #20 light green (B), #21 dark green (C), #28 turquoise (D) and #12 gold (E)
■ Size 2 (2.5mm) straight needles OR SIZE TO OBTAIN GAUGE
■ 1 set (4) size 2 (2.5mm) double pointed needles (dpn)
■ Stitch markers and stitch holders
■ Tapestry needle

GAUGE

33 sts and 40 rows to 4"/10cm over St st and argyle pat foll chart using size 2 (2.5mm) straight needles. TAKE TIME TO CHECK GAUGE.

STITCHES USED

K2, P2 Rib (multiple of 4 sts plus 2)
Row 1 (RS) K1 (selvage st), *k2, p2; rep from *, end k1 (selvage st).
Rep row 1 for k2, p2 rib.

CUFF

Beg at top edge with size 2 (2.5mm) straight needles and A, cast on 70 sts. Work in k2, p2 rib for 4½"/11.5cm, inc 1 st on last row—71 sts. Cont to work k1 selvage sts at beg and end of row, and rem sts in St st foll argyle chart for pat for 34 rows. Then work 1 more argyle rep only reversing B and C diamonds through row 34. Sock measures 11½"/29cm from beg. Adjust length at this point if desired.

INSTEP

Next row (RS) With A, k2tog, k16 then sl these 17 sts to a holder for heel; cont in argyle pat on center 35 sts (alternating C and B diamonds as before); sl last 18 sts to a holder for heel.
Cont in argyle pat on 35 sts for instep for 2 pat reps (68 rows). Cut yarn and leave instep sts on spare needle.

HEEL

Next row (WS) Rejoin A and p17 heel sts then p18 sts from other side to join heel at center—35 sts.
Next row (RS) Sl 1, k to end.
Next row Sl 1, p to end.
Rep last 2 rows until there are 32 rows in heel.

Turn heel

Next row (WS) Sl 1, p18, p2tog, p1, turn.

Row 2 Sl 1, k4, SKP, k1, turn.

Row 3 Sl 1, p5, p2tog, p1, turn.

Row 4 Sl, k6, SKP, k1, turn.

Cont to work in this way always having 1 more st before dec, and work SKP on RS rows or p2tog on WS rows, until there are 19 sts on heel needle. Cut yarn.

Shape gusset

With spare dpn and A, pick up and k 17 sts on right edge of heel, k10 sts of heel on same needle; with another dpn, k9 rem heel sts, then pick up and k 17 sts on left side of heel—53 sts. Working back and forth on these two needles in rows, work as foll with A:

Row 1 Purl.

Row 2 *Needle 1* K1, SKP, k to end; *Needle 2* k to last 3 sts, k2tog, k1.

Rep last 2 rows until there are 35 heel sts.

FOOT

Sl 35 sts onto one needle and work even with A in St st until there are same number of rows as in instep. Foot measures approx 8½"/21.5cm or 2"/5cm less than desired length from back of heel to end of toe. Make adjustments in length at this point (be sure to adjust instep length to correspond).

Shape toe

Beg at center of sole (the 35 heels sts in A), place sts on three dpn as foll: *Needle 1* 18 heel sts; *Needle 2* work the 18th heel st from *Needle 1* tog with the first instep st, work 33 instep sts; *Needle 3* work last instep st tog with next heel st, then work rem 16 sts—there are 17 sts on *Needle 1;* 34 sts on *Needle 2;* and 17 sts on *Needle 3*— 68 sts in total. Join, mark end of rnd and sl marker every rnd.

Rnd 1 Knit.

Rnd 2 *Needle 1* k to last 3 sts, k2tog, k1; *Needle 2* k1, SKP, k to last 3 sts, k2tog, k1; *Needle 3* k1, SKP, k to end.

Rep these 2 rnds until 20 sts rem. Divide sts on two needles and weave tog using Kitchener stitch.

FINISHING

Block socks lightly. If desired, embroider cross lines in duplicate stitch foll chart. Sew back and instep seams.

Color key

- Navy (A)
- Lt. Green (B)
- Dk. Green (C)
- Turquoise (D)
- Gold (E)

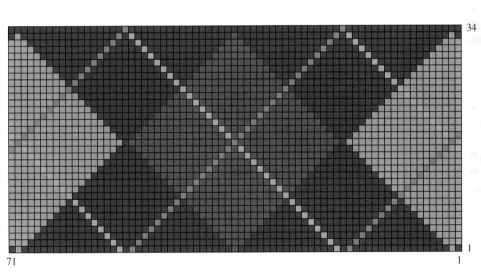

34

71

1

1

HEATHERED FAIR ISLE SOCKS

Muted shades of the Shetland Isles

Updated Fair Isle socks, designed by Petrea Noyes, feature clever turn-back cuffs. Heathered wool and delicate bands of traditional pattern draw upon a rich knitting heritage.

SIZES

Instructions are for woman's size Small. Changes for sizes Medium and Large are in parentheses.

MATERIALS

■ 2 1oz/30g skeins (each approx 150yd/138m) of Alice Starmore *Scottish Campion* (wool①) in #86 moorgrass (MC)
■ 1 skein each in #165 wood green (A), #31 corn (B), #59 olive (C), #80 mauve (D), #90 moss (E), #33 cream (F), #98 ochre (G), and #111 pine (H).
■ One pair straight needles each sizes 1 and 3 (2.25 and 3mm) OR SIZE TO OBTAIN GAUGE
■ One set (4) size 3 (3mm) double pointed needles (dpn)
■ Stitch markers
■ Tapestry needle

GAUGE

34 sts and 42 rows to 4"/10cm over Fair Isle pat foll chart using size 3 (3mm) needles. TAKE TIME TO CHECK GAUGE.

Note Cuff of sock in Fair Isle pat is worked back and forth in rows on two needles to heel. Then sts are joined and worked in rnds on dpn to end of sock.

CUFF

Beg at top edge with smaller straight needles and MC, cast on 72 sts. Work 3 rows in k1, p1 rib. Change to larger straight needles and p 1 row on WS. Then foll chart 1, and cont in St st, work 6-st rep of chart 12 times. Cont to row 9 of chart 1. With MC, p 1 row. Change to smaller straight needles.

Next row (RS) With MC, *k2tog, yo; rep from * to end (turning row for cuff). Change to larger straight needles.

Next row (RS) Knit.

Next row (WS) Purl.

Note RS and WS rows have switched for turn-back of cuff and work will cont in St st (k on RS, p on WS).

Cont with MC only for 14 more rows. Then foll chart 2, work 24-st rep 3 times and cont to row 47 (end of chart).

Next row (WS) With MC, purl, dec 12 (8, 6) sts evenly spaced—60 (64, 66) sts.

Join for heel

Using dpn, k15 (16, 16) sts on *Needle 1*, 30 (32, 33) sts (for instep) on *Needle 2*, and 15 (16, 17) sts on *Needle 3*. Join, taking care not to twist sts on needles. Mark end of rnd and sl marker every rnd. Cont with MC only, k 6 (10, 12) rnds.

HEEL

With spare needle, k15 (16, 16) sts from *Needle 1*, then sl 15 (16, 17) sts from *Needle 3* onto other end of same needle—30 (32, 33) heel sts. Divide rem 30 (32,

33) sts onto *Needle 2* and *Needle 3* to be worked later for instep. Work back and forth in St st and rows on heel sts only for 20 (20, 22) rows, end with a p row.

Turn heel

Next row K23 (24, 25), k2tog tbl, turn.

Row 2 Sl 1, p16 (16, 17), p2tog, turn.

Row 3 Sl 1, k16 (16, 17), k2tog tbl, turn.

Rep last 2 rows until all sts are worked and there are 18 (18, 19) heel sts.

Next rnd K9 sts and leave on needle. With spare needle, k9 (9, 10) sts (the rem sts of heel) with same needle pick up and k 15 (16, 17) sts along side of heel piece; with *Needle 2*, work across 30 (32, 33) instep sts; with *Needle 3* pick up and k 15 (16, 17) sts along other side of heel piece, with same needle k the rem 9 sts of heel— 78 (82, 86) sts.

Shape instep

Rnd 1 Knit.

Rnd 2 *Needle 1* k to last 2 sts, k2tog; *Needle 2* knit; *Needle 3* k2tog tbl, k to end. Rep last 2 rnds until there are 60 (64, 66) sts. Work even until foot measures 6 (7, 8)"/15.5 (17.5, 20.5)cm or 2"/5cm less than desired length from back of heel to end of toe.

Shape toe

Rnd 1 *Needle 1* k to last 3 sts, k2tog, k1; *Needle 2* k1, k2tog tbl, k to last 3 sts, k2tog, k1; *Needle 3* k1, k2tog tbl, k to end.

Rnd 2 Knit.

Rep these 2 rnds until 28 (28, 30) sts rem. Divide sts onto two needles and weave tog using Kitchener stitch.

FINISHING

Block socks. Sew back seam, folding at cuff and reversing seam for turn-back. Sew in ends neatly.

Color key

- Moorgrass (MC)
- Wood Green (A)
- Corn (B)
- Olive (C)
- Mauve (D)
- Moss (E)
- Cream (F)
- Ochre (G)
- Pine (H)

CHART 2

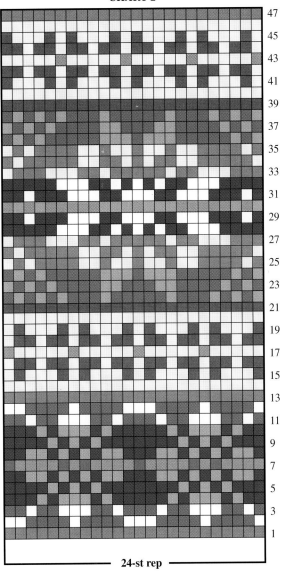

CHART 1

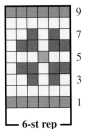

6-st rep

WIMBLEDON SOCKS

Tennis, anyone?

Classic woman's tennis socks designed by Mari Lynn Patrick. Choose a basic crew with athletic stripes or a footlet trimmed with contrasting pom-poms.

SIZES

Instructions are for woman's size 7½. Changes for sizes 8½, 9½ and 10½ are in parentheses.

MATERIALS

Crew Socks

■ 2 1¾oz/50g balls (each approx 195yd/180m) of Sesia *Sesia Baby* (cotton②) in #51 white (MC)
■ 1 ball in #109 lime (CC)

Footlets

■ 1 1¾oz/50g ball (each approx 195yd/180m) of Sesia *Sesia Baby* (cotton②) in #51 white (MC)
■ 1 ball in #109 lime (CC)

Both versions

■ One set (4) size 1 (2.25mm) double pointed needles (dpn) OR SIZE TO OBTAIN GAUGE
■ Size B/1 (2.00mm) crochet hook
■ Stitch markers
■ White elastic thread

GAUGE

32 sts and 42 rnds to 4"/10cm over St st using size 1 (2.25mm) needles. TAKE TIME TO CHECK GAUGE.

STITCHES USED

K2, P2 Rib

Row 1 (RS) *K2, p2; rep from * to end.
Row 2 (WS) K the knit sts and p the purl sts.
Rep row 2 for k2, p2 rib.

CREW SOCKS

Beg at top edge with MC and one needle, cast on 56 (60, 64, 68) sts. Divide sts on three needles as foll: 21 (22, 24, 25) sts on *Needle 1*; 14 (16, 16, 18) sts on *Needle 2*; 21 (22, 24, 25) sts on *Needle 3*. Join, taking care not to twist sts on needles. Mark end of rnd and sl marker every rnd. Work in k2, p2 rib for 5 rnds.

Next rnd With CC, knit. With CC, work 2 rnds in k2, p2 rib.

Next rnd With MC, knit. With MC, work 2 rnds in rib.

Next rnd With CC, knit.

Then cont with MC only in rib until piece measures 6"/15.5cm from beg.

HEEL

With spare needle, k14 (15, 16, 17) sts from *Needle 1*; then sl 14 (15, 16, 17) sts from *Needle 3* onto other end of spare needle—28 (30, 32, 34) sts for heel on spare needle. Divide rem 28 (30, 32, 34) sts on *Needle 2* and *Needle 3* to be worked later for instep. Work back and forth in rows on heel sts only.

Row 1 (WS) Sl 1, p to end.
Row 2 Sl 1, k to end.
Rep these 2 rows for 2 (2, 2¼, 2 ¼)"/5 (5,

5.75, 5.75)cm, end with a p row.

Turn heel

Next row K16 (17, 18, 19) sts (half the number of heel sts plus 2), k2tog, k1, turn.

Row 2 Sl 1, p5, p2tog, p1, turn.

Row 3 Sl 1, k6, k2tog, k1, turn.

Row 4 Sl 1, p7, p2tog, p1, turn.

Cont in this way, always having 1 more st before dec, and k2tog on RS rows or p2tog on WS rows, until there are 16 (18, 18, 20) sts on heel needle.

Next row K8 (9, 9, 10) sts and leave on needle. With spare needle, k8 (9, 9, 10) sts (the rem sts of heel), with same needle pick up and k 14 (15, 16, 17) sts along side of heel piece; with *Needle 2* work across 28 (30, 32, 34) instep sts; with *Needle 3* pick up and k 14 (15, 16, 17) sts along side of heel piece, with same needle k the rem 8 (9, 9, 10) sts of heel—72 (78, 82, 88) sts.

Shape instep

Rnd 1 K all sts.

Rnd 2 *Needle 1* k to last 3 sts, k2tog, k1; *Needle 2* knit; *Needle 3* k1, SKP, k to end of needle.

Rep these 2 rnds until there are 56 (60, 64, 68) sts on all three needles. Work even until foot measures 5 (6, 7, 8)"/12.5 (15.5, 17.5, 20.5)cm or 2"/5cm less than desired length from back of heel to end of toe.

Shape toe

Rnd 1 *Needle 1* k to last 3 sts, k2tog, k1; *Needle 2* k1, SKP, k to last 3 sts, k2tog, k1; *Needle 3* k1, SKP, k to end.

Rnd 2 Knit.

Rep these 2 rnds until there are 8 sts on *Needle 2*. Place sts from *Needle 1* and *Needle 3* on same needle. Cut yarn, leaving an end for sewing. Weave sts tog using Kitchener stitch. (OR, bind off using two needle method.)

FINISHING

Block socks, being careful not to stretch ribbing. Sew several rows of elastic thread through rows at sock top for best fit.

FOOTLETS

With MC, cast on and work as for crew socks for 4 rnds. Then, beg heel and cont same as for crew socks.

FINISHING

Block socks. Sew several rows of elastic thread through rib rows at sock top, adjusting for best fit. Working over elastic thread with crochet hook and 2 strands CC, working down into 3rd rib row, work sc (in each p rib) and ch 1, skip each k rib for trim. Make two pom-poms with CC. Fasten at back of sock.

BINDING OFF TWO PIECES TOGETHER

1 With RS placed together, hold pieces on two parallel needles. Insert a third needle knitwise into the first stitch of each needle, and wrap the yarn around the needle as if to knit.

2 Knit these two stitches together, and slip them off the needles. *Knit the next two stitches together in the same manner.

3 Slip the first stitch on the third needle over the second stitch and off the needle. Repeat from the * in step 2 across the row until all stitches have been bound off.

Variegated woolen socks with ribbed cuff, designed by Ruth Tobacco, feature an extra-easy heel and instep shaping. Knit tightly in a hefty yarn, they are set to become a winter basic.

SIZES

Instructions are for woman's size Medium. Changes for man's size Medium are in parentheses.

MATERIALS

- 3 1¾oz/50g balls (each approx 97yd/90m) of Ornaghi Filati/Trendsetter *Tundra* (wool/acrylic/polyester④) in #13 blue multi
- 1 set (5) size 6 (4mm) double pointed needles (dpn) OR SIZE TO OBTAIN GAUGE
- Stitch markers
- Tapestry needle

GAUGE

20 sts and 32 rnds to 4"/10cm over St st using size 6 (4mm) needles. TAKE TIME TO CHECK GAUGE.

CUFF

Beg at top edge cast on 44 sts on one needle. Divide sts onto four needles, with 11 sts on each needle. Join, taking care not to twist sts on needles. Mark end of rnd and sl marker every rnd.

Rnd 1 *K2, p2; rep from * around.
Rep rnd 1 for k2, p2 rib for 7½ (8½)"/19 (21.5)cm.

HEEL

Next rnd *K3, k2tog; rep from * 3 times more, k2. Place these 18 instep sts on a holder (or leave on needles) to be worked later. Work rem 22 sts for heel, back and forth in rows as foll:
Row 1 (RS) Sl 1 wyib, k21.
Row 2 Sl 1 wyif, p21.
Rep these 2 rows until heel measures 4"/10cm or desired length.

Heel seam
Bind off 22 sts loosely, leaving an end for sewing. With WS of heel tog, fold heel in half lengthwise. Sew tog bound-off sts to form heel seam.

INSTEP

Beg at top left side of heel and end at top right side, pick up and k 26 sts from side of heel, pm (for beg of rnd), k 18 sts from holder (divide 11 sts on each of four needles for a total of 44 sts). Work in rnds of St st (k every rnd) until foot measures 7½ (8½)"/19 (21.5)cm or 1½"/4cm less than desired length from back of heel to end of toe.

Shape toe
Next rnd *Needle 1* k1, SKP, k to end; *Needle 2* k to last 3 sts, k2tog, k1; *Needle 3* k1, SKP, k to end; *Needle 4* k to last 3 sts, k2tog, k1.
Rep this rnd until there are 4 sts on each needle—a total of 16 sts. Place sts on two needles and weave tog using Kitchener stitch.

BABY ARGYLES

First steps in sophisticated style

Classic argyle socks for the younger set, designed by Elsie Faulconer. These quick-to-knit tiny socks are a delightful introduction to argyle patterning. Duplicate stitch diamonds can be added after knitting.

SIZES

Instructions are for infant's size 3-6 months. Changes for sizes 9-12 months and 18-24 months are in parentheses.

MATERIALS

■ 1 1¾oz/50g ball (each approx 231yd/213m) each of Schoeller-Esslinger/Skacel *Fortissima Cotton* (cotton/synthetic②) in #57 light blue (A), #28 yellow (B), #16 dark blue (C)

■ 1 set (4) size 1 (2.25mm) double pointed needles (dpn) OR SIZE TO OBTAIN GAUGE

■ Stitch holders and markers

■ Tapestry needle

GAUGE

34 sts and 48 rows to 4"/10cm over St st and argyle pat foll chart using size 1 (2.25mm) needles. TAKE TIME TO CHECK GAUGE.

Notes 1 Cast on and work sock back and forth in rows on two needles to toe. Then join and work in rnds while shaping toe.

2 If desired, argyle cross lines may be embroidered in duplicate stitch after socks are knit.

CUFF

Beg at top edge with two needles and A, cast on 43 sts. Work in rows of k1, p1 rib for 10 rows.

Beg chart: Next row Foll chart row 1 for argyle diamond pat (cross lines may be worked in duplicate stitch after pieces are knit), work in pat for 22 rows.

Row 23 With A, k11 sts and sl to holder for half of heel, work 21 sts in pat, sl rem 11 sts to holder for 2nd half of heel. Then, working on 21 instep sts only, work chart pat through row 43. Work even with A for 0 (4, 10) rows more.

HEEL

With RS facing and A, k across heel sts from holders to join as foll: k to last st of 1st holder, k last st tog with first st on 2nd holder, k to end—21 sts.

Next row (WS) Purl.

Next row (RS) *Sl 1, k1; rep from * to end.

Rep these 2 rows for a total of 10 rows.

Turn heel

Next row (WS) P11, p2tog, p1, turn.

Row 2 K3, SKP, k1, turn.

Row 3 P4, p2tog, p1, turn.

Row 4 K5, SKP, k1, turn.

Cont in this way always having 1 more st before dec, and SKP on RS rows or p2tog on WS rows, until there are 11 sts on heel needle. Cut yarn.

GUSSET AND FOOT

With spare needle and A, pick up and k 8 sts on right edge of heel, k6 heel sts. With another needle, k5 rem heel sts then pick up and k 8 sts on left side of heel. Working back and forth in rows on these two needles, work as foll with A:

Row 1 (WS) Purl.

Row 2 *Needle 1* k1, SKP, k to end; *Needle 2* k to last 3 sts, k2tog, k1.

Rep these 2 rows until there are 21 heel sts. Then work even in St st until there are same number of rows as argyle instep.

Shape toe

Beg at center of sole (the 21 heel sts in A), place sts on three needles as foll: 11 sts on *Needle 1*; 21 sts on *Needle 2;* 10 sts on *Needle 3*. Place marker for beg of rnd and join to work in rnds.

Rnd 1 Knit.

Rnd 2 *Needle 1* k to last 3 sts, k2tog, k1; *Needle 2* k1, SKP, k to last 3 sts, k2tog, k1; *Needle 3* k1, SKP, k to end.

Rep these 2 rnds until 10 sts rem. Divide sts on two needles and weave tog using Kitchener stitch.

FINISHING

Block socks lightly. If desired, embroider cross lines in duplicate st foll chart. Sew back and instep seams.

Color key

▧ Light Blue (A)

☐ Yellow (B)

▓ Dark Blue (C)

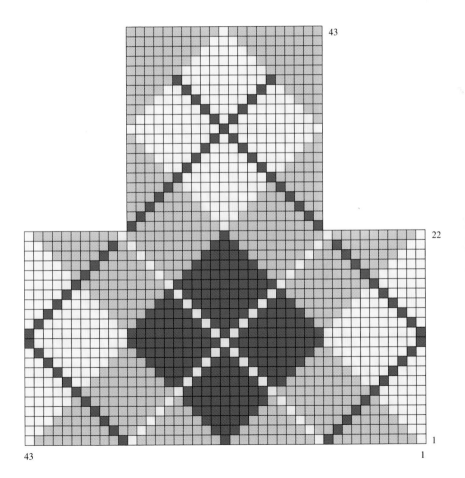

LUMBERJACK SOCKS
Northern exposure

Authentic Canadian woodsman's socks designed by Edward Bourgo and Gayle Hildebrandt. Special heel turn and ribbed ankle band keep them comfortable under workboots. "Phoenix Rising," the traditional symbol of choice, is emblazoned on the foot.

SIZES

Instructions are written for woman's size Medium. Adjustments may be made when working foot length to accommodate either man's or woman's sizes.

MATERIALS

- 2 1¾oz/50g balls (each approx 110yd/100m) of Cleckheaton *Machine Wash 8-Ply* by Plymouth Yarn (wool③) in #50 off white (MC)
- 1 ball each in #1960 tobacco (A), #1883 rust (B) and #1961 pumpkin (C)
- 1 set (4) size 4 (3.5mm) double pointed needles (dpn) OR SIZE TO OBTAIN GAUGE
- Stitch marker
- Tapestry needle

GAUGE

24 sts and 28 rows to 4"/10cm over St st using size 4 (3.5mm) needles. TAKE TIME TO CHECK GAUGE.

CUFF

Beg at top edge with MC, on one needle cast on 50 sts. Divide sts on three needles as foll: 16 sts on *Needle 1*; 18 sts on *Needle 2*; and 16 sts on *Needle 3*. Join, taking care not to twist sts on needles. Mark end of rnd and sl marker every rnd. Work in k1, p1 rib for 2"/5cm.

Next rnd With A, work in k1, p1 rib.

Next rnd With A, *k1, p1, k into front and back of next st (inc), p1; rep from * around, end k1, p1—62 sts.

Next rnd With A, *k1, p1, k2, p1; rep from *, end k1, p1.

Cont in rib as established for 3 more rnds with A, 6 rnds with B, 4 rnds with C, 6 rnds with B, 6 rnds with A, 3 rnds with MC. Then cont with MC only as foll:

Next rnd K1, p1, k2tog, p1, work rib to last 5 sts, k2tog, p1, k1, p1—60 sts.

Work even in rib as established for 7 rnds.

Next rnd [K1, p1] 3 times, k2tog, work rib to last 9 sts, k2tog, rib to end.

Work in rib for 6 rnds. Cont to dec in this way by working k2tog in first k2 rib at beg of rnd and k2tog in last k2 rib at end of rnd every 6th rnd once, every 5th rnd once, every 4th rnd once, then every 3rd rnd once—50 sts. Cont in k1, p1 rib until leg measures 11"/28cm or desired length.

HEEL

Divide sts as foll: sl last 12 sts from *Needle 3* onto end of *Needle 1*, then sl 4 sts from other end of *Needle 1* onto *Needle 2*—24 heel sts on *Needle 1*. Divide rem 26 sts onto two needles to be worked later for instep.

Row 1 (RS) Sl 1, *k1, sl 1; rep from *, end k1.

Rows 2 and 4 Sl 1, p to end.

Row 3 Sl 1, k2, *sl 1, k1; rep from *, end k1.

Rep these 4 rows for heel pat until heel measures 2¼"/5.75cm.

Turn heel

Next row K14, k2tog, k1, turn.

Row 2 Sl 1, p5, p2tog, p1, turn.

Row 3 Sl 1, k6, k2tog, k1, turn.

Row 4 Sl 1, p7, p2tog, p1, turn.

Cont in this way always having 1 more st before dec, and k2tog on RS rows or p2tog on WS rows, until there are 14 heel sts.

GUSSET

Next rnd K7 sts and leave on needle, with spare needle k7 (the rem sts of heel) with same needle pick up and k 18 sts along side of heel piece (*Needle 1*); *Needle 2* work across 26 instep sts; *Needle 3* pick up and k 18 sts along other side of heel piece, k the rem 7 sts of heel—76 sts.

Shape instep

Rnd 1 *Needle 1* k to last 2 sts, SKP; *Needle 2* knit; *Needle 3* SSK, k to end. Rep this rnd 12 times more—50 sts.

Divide sts on three needles as foll: 16 sts on *Needle 1*; 18 sts on *Needle 2*; and 16 sts on *Needle 3*. Work even for 4 rnds. Then beg foll chart 1 for phoenix pat, centering row 1 on center of instep.

Note Foll rnds 1-19 of chart 1 for right sock; foll rnds 1-7 of chart 1-a, then cont rnds 8-19 of chart 1 for left sock.

After chart is completed, work 1 rnd even with MC. Then work chart 2, working 10-st rep 5 times. When chart is completed, work even with MC until foot measures 7"/18cm or 2"/5cm less than desired length from back of heel to end of toe.

Shape toe

Rnd 1 *Needle 1* k to last 3 sts, k2tog, k1; *Needle 2* k1, SKP, k to last 3 sts, k2tog, k1; *Needle 3* k1, SKP, k to end.

Rnd 2 Knit.

Rep these 2 rnds until there are 6 sts on *Needle 2*. Place sts on two needles and weave tog using Kitchener stitch.

FINISHING

Block socks, including light blocking of leg ribbing. Sew in ends neatly.

Color key

☐ Off-white (MC)

▨ Tobacco (A)

■ Brick (B)

CHART 1-a

CHART 1

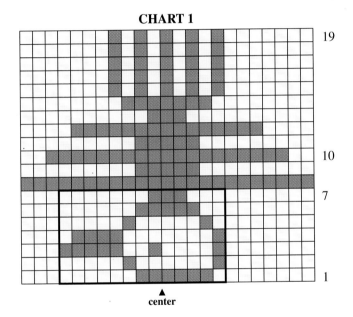

CHART 2

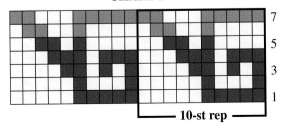

ZIG ZAG SOCKS

Subtle colorwork takes a new direction

Cleverly patterned from top to toe, these socks, designed by Shannon Stoney, feature alternating background and foreground coloring. Bi-color ribbing at the cuff lends visual impact.

SIZES

Instructions are written for woman's size Medium.

MATERIALS

■ 1 1¾oz/50g ball (each approx 215yd/196m) of Brown Sheep *Wildfoote* (wool/nylon②) each in #SY30 purple (A), #SY11 camel (B), #SY22 blue (C) and #SY20 plum (D)
■ 1 set (5) size 2 (2.5mm) double pointed needles (dpn) OR SIZE TO OBTAIN GAUGE
■ Stitch marker
■ Tapestry needle

GAUGE

36 sts and 36 rows to 4"/10cm over St st and chart pat using size 2 (2.5mm) needles. TAKE TIME TO CHECK GAUGE.

Notes I When changing colors, twist yarns on WS to prevent holes.
2 Seam of sock cuff will be at side of heel, not center of heel.

CUFF

Beg at top edge with A, on one needle cast on 76 sts. Divide sts on three needles as foll: 28 sts on *Needle 1*; 20 sts on *Needle 2*; 28 sts on *Needle 3*. Join, taking care not to twist sts on needles. Mark end of rnd and sl marker every rnd.
Rnd I With A, *k2, p2; rep from * around.
Rnds 2-8 *K2 with A, p2 with B; rep from * around.
Rnds 9 and 10 *K2 with A, p2 with D; rep from * around.
Then work in St st and foll chart 1 beg with rnd 11, working 4-st rep 19 times. Cont to foll chart through rnd 35. Piece measures approx 4"/10cm from beg.

HEEL

For right sock

Sl 28 sts from *Needle 1* and 10 sts from beg of *Needle 2* onto spare needle for heel, divide rem 38 sts with 19 sts each on *Needle 2* and *Needle 3* to be worked later for instep.

For left sock

Sl 28 sts from *Needle 3* and 10 sts from end of *Needle 2* onto spare needle for heel, divide rem 38 sts with 19 sts each on *Needle 2* and *Needle 3* to be worked later for instep.

For both socks

Work back and forth in rows (beg with a p row, then k 1 row, p 1 row) on 38 heel sts only, cont in pat through row 65. Heel piece measures approx 3½"/9cm long.

Turn heel

Work heel in last 2 colors (B and C) and 2-color pat foll chart 2, work as foll:
Row I (RS) Sl 1, k18, SSK, k1, turn.

Row 2 Sl 1, p1, p2tog, p1, turn.

Row 3 Sl 1, k2, SSK, k1, turn.

Row 4 Sl 1, p3, p2tog, p1, turn.

Cont in this way always having 1 more st before dec, and work SSK on RS rows or p2tog on WS rows, until all sts are worked and there are 20 sts on heel needle.

Shape gusset

Note When working chart 2, work 2-color pat with same 2 colors used in chart 1.

Next rnd *Needle 1* sl 1, cont chart 2, k19 (heel sts), with same needle pick up and k 21 sts along side of heel piece (cont chart 2); *Needle 2* and *Needle 3* cont in color pat foll chart 1 on 38 sts beg with rnd 36; *Needle 4* working in chart 2 pat, pick up and k 21 sts along other side of heel piece, then k10 from *Needle 1*—100 sts total. Seam is now at center of heel or sole of sock. Cont to work sts on *Needle 1* and *Needle 4* in chart 2 and 38 instep sts (*Needle 2* and *Needle 3*) in chart 1 as before.

Rnd 2 *Needle 1* k to last 2 sts, k2tog; *Needle 2* and *Needle 3* work even in pat foll chart; *Needle 4* SSK, k to end.

Rnd 3 Work even foll chart 1 for instep and chart 2 for sole sts.

Rep last 2 rnds until there are 19 sts on all four needles—76 sts. Work even in charts 1 and 2 as established until foot measures 6"/15.25cm or 2½"/6.5cm less than desired length from back of heel to end of toe.

Shape toe

Note Work chart 1 on all four needles while shaping toe.

Rnd 1 *Needle 1* k to last 4 sts, k2tog, k2; *Needle 2* k2, SSK, k to end; *Needle 3* k to last 4 sts, k2tog, k2; *Needle 4* k2, SSK, k to end.

Rnd 2 Knit.

Rep last 2 rnds until 24 sts rem (6 sts on each needle). Divide sts onto two needles and weave tog using Kitchener stitch.

FINISHING

Block socks being careful not to flatten rib. Weave in ends neatly.

Color key

■ Purple (A)

☐ Camel (B)

■ Blue (C)

■ Plum (D)

Color key

☐ Color 1

■ Color 2

CHART 2

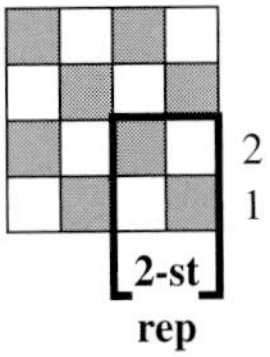

2
1

2-st rep

CHART 1

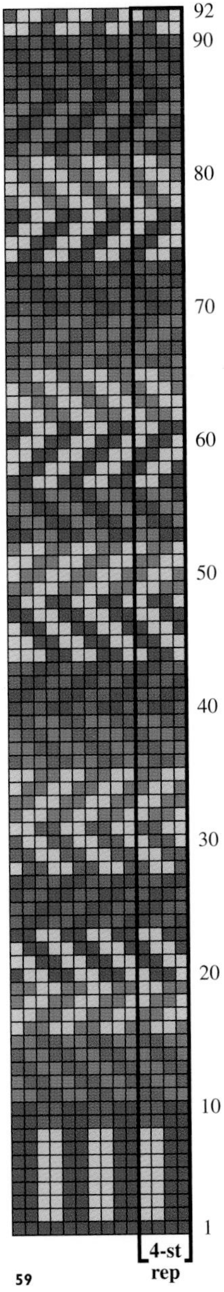

92
90

80

70

60

50

40

30

20

10

1

4-st rep

59

LADYBUG SOCKS

Summer charmers for tiny toes

Baby socks with a bright band of lady-bugs at the cuff, designed at the Dale of Norway Studio. Delightfully fresh colors and Fleur-de-Lis patterning on the foot add to the charm.

SIZES

Instructions are for infant's size 3-6 months. Changes for 9-12 and 18-24 months are in parentheses.

MATERIALS

■ 1 1¾oz/50g skein (each approx 189yd/175m) of Dale of Norway *Baby Wool* (wool①) each in #2908 orange (MC), #3718 red (A), #8523 green (B), #5755 navy (C)
■ 1 set (4) each sizes 0 and 2 (2 and 2.5mm) double pointed needles (dpn) OR SIZE TO OBTAIN GAUGE
■ Stitch holders and markers

GAUGE

30 sts and 32 rnds to 4"/10cm over St st and chart pats using larger needles. TAKE TIME TO CHECK GAUGE.
Note When changing colors, twist yarns on WS to prevent holes.

CUFF

Beg at top edge with A, cast on 44 (48, 48) sts on one smaller needle. Divide sts onto three smaller needles with 14 (16, 16) sts on *Needle 1*, and 15 (16, 16) sts each on *Needle 2* and *Needle 3*. Join, taking care not to twist sts on needles. Mark end of rnd and sl marker every rnd. Work in rnds of k1, p1 rib for ¾"/2cm. Change to larger needles.

Beg chart 1: Rnd 1 Foll chart 1 for ladybug pat, work 9-st rep 4 (0, 0) times, 8-st rep 1 (6, 6) times. Work through rnd 12 of chart.

HEEL

With MC, k22 (24, 24) sts for heel, sl rem sts onto a holder for instep. Work back and forth in rows and St st (k 1 row, p 1 row) on heel sts only for 1 (1⅛, 1⅛)"/2.5 (3, 3)cm, end with a p row.

Turn heel

Next row (RS) K13 (14, 14) sts (half the number of heel sts plus 2), k2tog tbl, k1, turn.

Row 2 Sl 1, p5, p2tog, p1, turn.
Row 3 Sl 1, k6, k2tog tbl, k1, turn.
Row 4 Sl 1, p7, p2tog, p1, turn.
Row 5 Sl 1, k8, k2tog tbl, k1, turn.

Cont in this way, always having 1 more st before dec, and k2tog tbl on RS rows or p2tog on WS rows, until all sts are worked, end with a p row.

Shape instep

With MC, knit first half of heel sts (7 sts) and sl to end of *Needle 3*, k 2nd half of heel sts (7 sts) onto *Needle 1*, then with same needle, pick up and k 8 (9, 9) sts along side of heel; with *Needle 2* k 22 (24, 24) sts from instep holder; with *Needle 3* pick up and k 8 (9, 9) sts along side of heel, k rem sts—15 (16, 16) sts each on *Needle 1* and *Needle 3* and a total of 52 (56, 56) sts. Mark center heel for beg of rnds.

Next rnd *Needle 1* work pat foll chart 2 to last 2 sts, k2tog; *Needle 2* work even foll chart 2; *Needle 3* SSK, work chart 2 to end.

Rep this rnd until there are 42 (48, 48) sts. Work even in chart 2 until foot measures 2½ (2¾, 3¼)"/6.5 (7, 8.25)cm or 1½"/4cm less than desired length from back of heel to end of toe.

Shape toe

Next rnd With MC only, *Needle 1* k to last 3 sts, k2tog, k1; *Needle 2* k1, k2tog tbl, k to last 3 sts, k2tog, k1; *Needle 3* k1, k2tog tbl, k to end.

Rep this rnd every rnd until 8 sts rem. Thread yarn through rem sts and pull through to tighten. Fasten off.

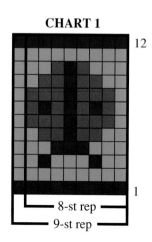

Color key

Orange (MC)

Red (A)

Green (B)

Navy (C)

CHART 1

12

1

8-st rep

9-st rep

CHART 2

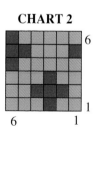

6

1

6   1

GIRL'S LACY SOCKS

Pretty in peach

Lace socks with vertical eyelet pattern stripes, designed by Lila P. Chin. Just right for little feet, these dainty anklets feature turn-back cuffs with picot edging.

SIZES

Instructions are for girl's size X-Small (4-5½). Changes for sizes Small (5-6½) and Medium (6-7½) are in parentheses.

MATERIALS

■ 1 1¾oz/50g ball (each approx 219yd/203m) of Lang/Berroco *BÉBÉ Lang Superwash* (wool②) in #7165 peach
■ 1 set (4) size 3 (3mm) double pointed needles (dpn) OR SIZE TO OBTAIN GAUGE
■ Stitch markers
■ Tapestry needle

GAUGE

7.5 sts and 10 rnds to 1"/2.5cm over lace chart using size 3 (3mm) needles. TAKE TIME TO CHECK GAUGE.

CUFF

Beg at top edge on one needle, cast on 42 sts. Divide sts evenly onto three needles—14 sts on each needle. Join, taking care not to twist sts on needles. Mark end of rnd and sl marker every rnd. Work in reverse St st (p every rnd) for 1"/2.5cm.
Next rnd *P2tog, yo; rep from * around (end of hem). Cont in reverse St st until

piece measures 2"/5cm from beg.
Next rnd *P2tog, yo; rep from * around. P 1 rnd. Then work in k1, p1 rib for ½"/1.25cm. Work in lace pat foll chart (one 14-st rep on each needle) until 3"/7.5cm from beg of lace pat, end with lace pat rnd 5 and dec 1 st at end of rnd—41 sts.

HEEL

Work rnd 6 ending with 6th st on *Needle 3*. Sl the 6 sts just worked onto *Needle 2* and last st from *Needle 1* onto *Needle 2*—21 instep sts. With spare needle, divide these 21 sts evenly onto two needles and leave to work later for instep. Return to 7 sts of *Needle 3* and work these sts plus 13 sts from *Needle 1*—20 heel sts. Work back and forth in rows on heel sts only.
Row 1 (WS) Sl 1 purlwise, p to end.
Row 2 (RS) Sl 1, *k1, sl 1; rep from *, end k1.
Rep these 2 rows until heel measures 1¼"/3cm, end with RS row.
Turn heel
Next row (WS) P12, p2tog, p1, turn.
Row 2 Sl 1, k5, SSK, k1, turn.
Row 3 Sl 1, p6, p2tog, p1, turn.
Row 4 Sl 1, k7, SSK, k1, turn.
Cont to work short rows in this way until all sts have been worked, end with a RS row—12 sts.

INSTEP

Sl last 6 sts of heel to spare needle then cont to pick up and k (with same needle) 11 sts from side of heel—17 sts on *Needle 1*;

work next 21 sts of instep resuming lace pat on 19 sts (sts 1-14 of chart, then sts 1-5 once more)—21 sts on *Needle 2*; with spare needle, pick up and k 12 sts from other side of heel and work across rem 6 sts of *Needle 1*—18 sts on *Needle 3* and a total of 56 sts.

Shape instep

Rnd 1 K all sts.

Rnd 2 *Needle 1* k to last 3 sts, SSK, k1; *Needle 2* work in chart pat; *Needle 3* k1, k2tog, k to end of needle.

Rep these 2 rnds until there are 42 sts on all three needles. Then work even in pats on all needles until foot measures 3¼ (4, 5)"/8.25 (10, 12.5)cm from beg of heel.

Shape toe

Rnd 1 *Needle 1* k to last 3 sts, SSK, k1; *Needle 2* k1, k2tog, k to last 3 sts, SSK, k1; *Needle 3* k1; k2tog, k to end.

Rnd 2 Knit.

Rep these 2 rnds until 18 sts rem. Divide sts on two needles and weave tog using Kitchener stitch.

FINISHING

Block lightly. Turn hem under and sew in place. Fold eyelet cuff down over sock.

Stitch key

I	k on RS
O	yarn over
⊼	k2tog
⋋	ssk

LACE CHART

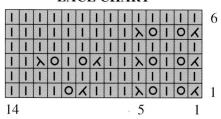

14   5   1

CABLED KNEE-HIGHS

A new slant on sock shaping

Cabled woman's knee-highs, designed by Norah Gaughan. Variations include slanted ridges or eyelets; special shaping techniques follow the contours of the calf.

SIZE

Instructions are written and charted for woman's size Medium/Long. Chart indicates areas to shorten calf length.

MATERIALS

Summer Socks

■ 4 1¾oz/50g balls (each approx 104yd/96m) of Unger *Sherbet* (cotton/microfiber③) in #4 pistachio

Winter Socks

■ 5 1¾oz/50g balls (each approx 96yd/88m) of Unger *Darby* (wool/acrylic④) in #10 steel heather

Both versions

■ One set (4) each sizes 2 and 4 (2.5 and 3.5mm) double pointed needles (dpn) OR SIZE TO OBTAIN GAUGE

■ Cable needle

■ Several yds of waste yarn

■ Stitch markers

■ Tapestry needle

GAUGE

23 sts and 32 rnds to 4"/10cm over St st using larger needles. TAKE TIME TO CHECK GAUGE.

Notes 1 Chart is for summer socks. To work winter socks, work the darker shaded symbols as foll: ⊠⃞⃞ as left twist (LT): ⃞⃞⊠ as right twist (RT).

2 Heel is worked separately after sock is completed by knitting heel sts first with waste yarn then returning to work heel sts only.

STITCH GLOSSARY

Right Twist (RT)
K2tog, k first st again, remove both from LH needle.

Left Twist (LT)
Skip first st and k through back of 2nd st, k through back of 1st and 2nd sts tog.

2/2 Right Cable (2/2RC)
Sl 2 sts to cn and hold to *back*, k2, then k2 from cn.

2/2 Left Cable (2/2LC)
Sl 2 sts to cn and hold to *front*, k2, then k2 from cn.

2/1 Right Yarnover Cross (2/1RYC)
Sl 1 st to cn and hold to *back*, k2, then yo, k1 from cn. (On next rnd, k into back of yo.)

2/1 Left Yarnover Cross (2/1LYC)
Sl 2 sts to cn and hold to *front*, k1, yo, then k2 from cn. (On next rnd, k into back of yo.)

2/2 Right Purl Cross (2/2RPC)
Sl 2 sts to cn and hold to *back*, k2, p2 from cn.

2/2 Left Purl Cross (2/2LPC)
Sl 2 sts to cn and hold to *front*, p2, k2 from cn.

2/2 Right Dec Cable (RDC)
Sl 2 sts to cn and hold to *back*, k2, then p2tog from cn.
2/2 Left Dec Cable (LDC)
Sl 2 sts to cn and hold to *front*, p2tog, k2 from cn.
4 x 4
Rep the 4 sts in this section 4 times.

CUFF

Beg at top edge, cast on 64 sts. Divide sts on three needles with 21 sts on *Needle 1*; 21 sts on *Needle 2*; 22 sts on *Needle 3*. Join, taking care not to twist sts on needles. Mark end of rnd and sl marker every rnd. Work around in k1, p1 rib for 1¼"/3cm.

Next rnd Change to larger needles and k this rnd, dec 1 st on *Needle 1*, dec 1 st on *Needle 2* and dec 2 sts on *Needle 3*—60 sts (20 sts on each of three needles).

Beg chart pat: Rnd 1 Foll rnd 1 of chart pat as foll: k4, p2, yo, SSK, k2, yo, SSK, [k2, yo, SSK] 4 times, k2, LT, RT, k2, [k2tog, yo, k] 4 times, k2tog, yo, k2, k2tog, yo, p2.

Cont to foll chart through rnd 107 (shorten calf if desired as indicated on chart). There are 48 sts after all decs and leg measures approx 14¾"/37.5cm from beg.

Next rnd *Needle 1* work 16 sts in St st (k every rnd); *Needle 2* 16 sts in chart rep (foll rows 108-123); *Needle 3* 16 sts in St st. (Sock will cont to be worked in this way to toe shaping.)

Rep last rnd 4 times more.

Next rnd Work 32 sts (to end of *Needle 2*), work first 4 sts of *Needle 3*, cut working yarn, then with waste yarn work next 24 sts for heel (including 12 sts from *Needle 1*). Cut waste yarn, rejoin working yarn, then cont in rnds on all 48 sts with 16 sts on each of three needles in original positions and instep pat on 16 sts, until foot measures 5"/12.5cm from waste yarn row, or 3"/7.5cm less than desired length from back of heel to end of toe.

Shape toe
Place a marker between 3rd and 4th sts before instep pat and between 3rd and 4th sts after instep pat. Then cont toe in St st only as foll:

Rnd 1 *K to 4 sts before marker, SSK, k2, k2tog; k to 4 sts before 2nd marker, SSK, k2, k2tog, k to end of rnd.

Rnd 2 Knit.

Rep last 2 rnds 5 times more. Divide rem 24 sts onto two needles and weave tog using Kitchener stitch.

HEEL

Return to sts on waste yarn and remove waste yarn carefully, placing open sts and lps onto two needles—there are 24 sts on one side and 25 lps on the other side. Beg in one corner, pick up and k 1 st in corner and mark this corner st, k across 12 sts with same needle; then with *Needle 1* k12 rem sts to corner, pick up and k 1 st in corner, k next 4 sts with same needle; with *Needle 2* k next 17 sts; with *Needle 3* k rem 4 sts and 13 sts from beg—51 sts and 17 sts on each of three needles.

Shape heel

Dec rnd K to 1 st before first corner st, k3tog, k to 1 st before 2nd corner st, k3tog, k to end.

Next rnd Knit.

Rep these 2 rnds 5 times more—27 sts.

Next rnd K to within 2 sts of corner st, SSK, k to end—26 sts.

Place 13 sts on each of two needles and weave tog using Kitchener stitch.

Stitch key

- ☐ k on RS, p on WS
- ☐ p on RS, k on WS
- ■ no stitch
- ☐ yarn over
- ☒ & ☒ k2tog
- ☒ & ☒ ssk
- ☒ RT
- ☒ LT
- ☒ 2/2 RC
- ☒ 2/2 LC
- ☒ 2/1 RYC
- ☒ 2/1 LYC
- ☒ 2/2 RPC
- ☒ 2/2 LPC
- ☒ 2/2 RDC
- ☒ 2/2 LDC

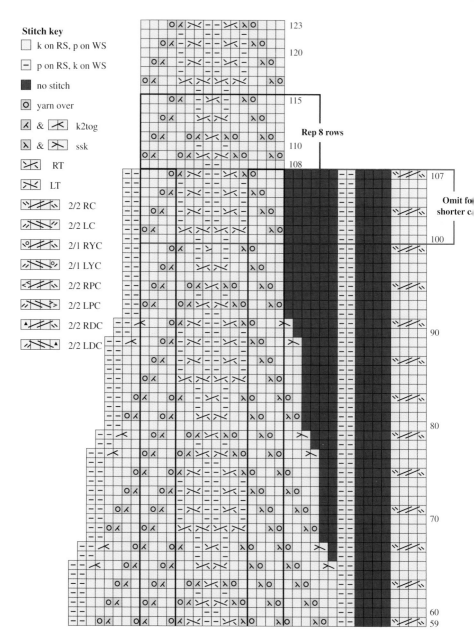

Rep 8 rows

Omit for shorter ca

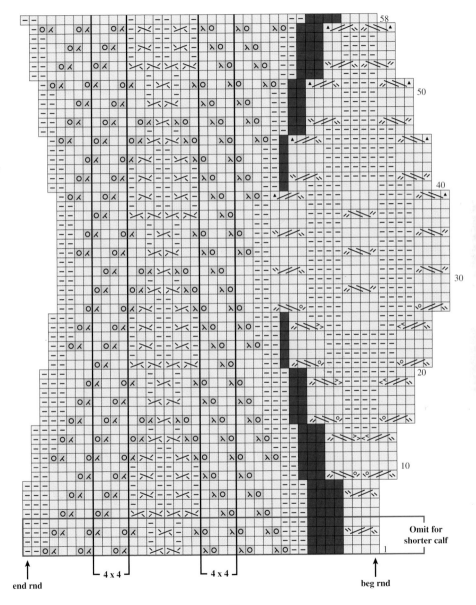

58

50

40

30

20

10

1

Omit for
shorter calf

4 x 4

4 x 4

end rnd

beg rnd

71

NORDIC KNEE-HIGHS

Bright ideas for little feet

Two-color Nordic-motif socks, designed at the Dale of Norway Studio. Created just for kids, special shaping keeps these brightly patterned knee socks from sliding down little legs.

SIZES

Instructions are for child's size 2 years. Changes for sizes 4, 6 and 8 years are in parentheses.

MATERIALS

Red Socks
■ 1 (2, 2, 3) 1¾oz/50g balls (each approx 189yd/175m) of Dale of Norway *Baby Wool* (wool①) in #3718 red (MC)
■ 1 ball in #2908 orange (CC)

Blue Socks
■ 1 (2, 2, 3) 1¾oz/50g balls (each approx 189yd/175m) of Dale of Norway *Baby Wool* (wool①) in #5545 blue (MC)
■ 1 ball in #7436 green (CC)

Both versions
■ 1 set (4) size 2 (2.5mm) double pointed needles (dpn) OR SIZE TO OBTAIN GAUGE
■ Stitch markers

GAUGE

34 sts and 36 rnds to 4"/10cm over St st and chart pat using size 2 (2.5mm) needles. TAKE TIME TO CHECK GAUGE.

Note When changing colors, twist yarns on WS to prevent holes.

CUFF

Beg at top edge with MC, on one needle cast on 60 (68, 76, 84) sts. Divide sts on three needles as foll: 20 (24, 26, 28) sts on *Needle 1*; 20 (20, 24, 28) sts on *Needle 2*; 20 (24, 26, 28) sts on *Needle 3*. Join, taking care not to twist sts on needles. Mark end of rnd and sl marker every rnd. Work in rnds of k1, p1 rib for 1½ (2, 2, 2¼)"/4 (5, 5, 6)cm, inc 4 sts evenly on last rnd—64 (72, 80, 88) sts.

Next rnd Work 8 sts foll chart 1, 48 (56, 64, 72) sts foll chart 2, end with st 16 (8, 16, 8), beg with CC (MC, CC, MC), work rem 8 sts foll chart 1.

Work even for 2 rnds more. Dec 1 st at beg and end of next rnd and rep dec every 5th rnd 7 (9, 11, 13) times more. Work even in pat on 48 (52, 56, 60) sts until leg measures 7 (7¾, 9¼, 10¼)"/18 (19.5, 23.5, 26)cm.

HEEL

With MC only and spare needle, k12 (13, 14, 15) sts from *Needle 1*, then sl last 12 (13, 14, 15) sts from end of *Needle 3* onto other end of spare needle—24 (26, 28, 30) heel sts. Divide rem 24 (26, 28, 30) sts on *Needle 2* and *Needle 3* to be worked later for instep. With MC, work back and forth in rows on heel sts only for 1⅛ (1⅜, 1½, 1¾)"/3 (3.5, 4, 4.5)cm.

Turn heel

Next row (RS) K14 (16, 18, 20), k2tog tbl, k1, turn.

Row 2 (WS) Sl 1, p5 (7, 9, 11), p2tog, p1, turn.

Row 3 Sl 1, k6 (8, 10, 12), k2tog tbl, k1, turn.

Row 4 Sl 1, p7 (9, 11, 13), p2tog, p1, turn. Cont in this way always having 1 more st before dec, and k2tog tbl on RS rows or p2tog on WS rows, until all sts have been worked—14 (16, 18, 20) heel sts.

Next rnd K7 (8, 9, 10) sts and leave on needle. With spare needle, k7 (8, 9, 10) (the rem sts of heel), with same needle pick up and k 9 (9, 10, 11) sts along side of heel piece; with *Needle 2* work across 24 (26, 28, 30) instep sts; with *Needle 3* pick up and k 9 (9, 10, 11) sts along other side of heel piece, with same needle, k the rem 7

(8, 9, 10) sts of heel—56 (60, 66, 72) sts.

Shape instep

Rnd 1 Knit.

Rnd 2 *Needle 1* k to last 2 sts, k2tog; *Needle 2* knit; *Needle 3* SKP, k to end. Rep last (dec) rnd every rnd until there are 48 (52, 56, 60) sts. Work even until foot measures 3½ (4, 4¾, 5⅛)"/9 (10, 12, 13)cm or 1¼"/3cm less than desired length from back of heel to end of toe.

Shape toe

Rnd 1 *Needle 1* k to last 2 sts, SKP; *Needle 2* k2tog, k to last 2 sts, SKP; *Needle 3* k2tog, k to end. Rep this rnd every rnd until 4 sts rem. Cut yarn and pull through rem sts and fasten.

FINISHING

Block socks. Sew in ends neatly.

CHART 2

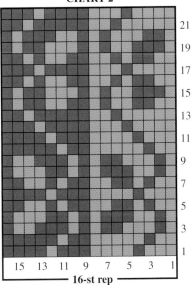

21
19
17
15
13
11
9
7
5
3
1

15   13   11   9   7   5   3   1

16-st rep

Color key

Red (MC)

Orange (CC)

CHART 1

7   5   3   1

8-st rep

CHART 2

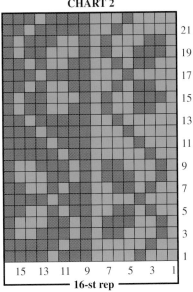

21
19
17
15
13
11
9
7
5
3
1

15   13   11   9   7   5   3   1

16-st rep

Color key

Blue (MC)

Green (CC)

CHART 1

7   5   3   1

8-st rep

HOLLY LEAF SOCKS

Deck your toes in socks of holly

Leaves, berries and cozy cabled ribs decorate Sasha Kagan's woman's socks. Tweedy yarns and chenille bobble berries add to the textural appeal.

SIZES

Instructions are for woman's size Medium. Changes for size Large are in parentheses.

MATERIALS

- 3 .8oz/25g balls (each approx 110yd/100m) of Rowan *Donegal Lambswool* (wool②) in #485 bay green (MC)
- 1 ball each in #479 cinnamon (A) and #487 grey (B)
- 1 .8oz/25g ball (each approx 75yd/67m) of *Lightweight DK* (wool②) in #134 medium green (C)
- 1 1¾oz/50g ball (each approx 173yd/160m) of *Fine Cotton Chenille* (cotton/polyester④) in #406 red (D)
- 1 set (4) each sizes 2 and 3 (2.5 and 3mm) double pointed needles (dpn) OR SIZE TO OBTAIN GAUGE
- Stitch holders and markers
- Tapestry needle

GAUGE

33 sts and 36 rows to 4"/10cm over St st and chart pat using larger needles. TAKE TIME TO CHECK GAUGE.

Note Cast on and work sock back and forth in rows on two needles to toe. Then join and work in rnds while shaping toe.

STITCHES USED

Mock Cable Rib (multiple of 4 sts plus 2)

Row 1 (RS) *P2, skip 1 st and k into 2nd st, then k into first st and sl both sts off needle (2-st twist); rep from *, end p2.

Row 2 *K2, p2; rep from *, end k2.

Row 3 *P2, k2; rep from *, end p2.

Row 4 Rep row 2.

Rep rows 1-4 for mock cable rib.

Chart Pattern

Work color pat foll chart in St st using intarsia method: Work each separate section of color with a separate length or bobbin of yarn and twist yarns on WS when changing colors to avoid holes.

Bobble

Make bobble as indicated on chart as foll: K into front and back of st, turn, k2, turn, p2, turn, k2tog.

CUFF

Beg at top edge with two smaller needles and A, cast on 74 sts. Work 1 row in mock cable pat. Then change to MC and cont in mock cable pat until piece measures 2"/5cm from beg. Change to larger needles.

Beg chart pat: Row 1 (RS) Cont 26 sts in mock cable pat with MC, k1 with MC, work 20 sts chart pat, k1 with MC, cont 26 sts in mock cable pat with MC. Cont in this way until row 48 of chart is completed.

Divide for instep
Next row (RS) Work 55 sts in pat, turn, sl last 19 sts to a holder.

Next row Work 36 sts in pat, turn, sl rem 19 sts to a holder. Cont on these 36 instep sts in established pats for 39 (48) chart rows more. Leave these sts on a spare needle for instep to be worked later.

HEEL
Rejoin MC and with RS facing, sl sts from both holders onto one needle with back of leg seam at center—38 heel sts. Work 20 rows in mock cable rib.

Turn heel
Row 1 (RS) K28, SKP, turn.
Row 2 P19, p2tog, turn.
Row 3 K19, SKP, turn.
Row 4 Rep row 2.
Rep last 2 rows until 20 sts rem, end with a p row. Cut yarn.

Shape gusset
With spare needle and MC, pick up and k 16 sts on right edge of heel, k10 sts of heel on same needle; with another needle, k rem 10 heel sts, then pick up and k 16 sts on left side of heel—52 sts. Working back and forth on these two needles in rows,

with MC work as foll:
Row 1 Purl.
Row 2 K1, SKP, k to last 3 sts, k2tog, k1.
Row 3 K1, p to last st, k1.
Rep last 2 rows until there are 40 heel sts.

FOOT
Sl 40 sts onto one needle and work even in St st with MC until there are same number of rows as in instep. Foot measures approx 4½ (5½)"/11.5 (14)cm or 2"/5cm less than desired length from back of heel to end of toe. Make adjustments at this point, if desired.

Shape toe
Beg at center of sole (the 40 heel sts in MC), place 76 sts on three needles as foll: 19 sts on *Needle 1*; 38 sts on *Needle 2*; 19 sts on *Needle 3*. Place marker for beg of rnd and join to work in rnds.
Rnd 1 Knit.
Rnd 2 *Needle 1* k to last 3 sts, k2tog, k1; *Needle 2* k1, SKP, k to last 3 sts, k2tog, k1; *Needle 3* k1, SKP, k to end.
Rep these 2 rnds until 32 sts rem. Divide sts on two needles and weave tog using Kitchener stitch.

FINISHING
Block socks lightly. Sew back and instep seams.

Color key

■ Bay Green (MC)

▨ Cinnamon (A)

□ Grey (B)

▨ Medium Green (C)

● Red (D)
Bobble

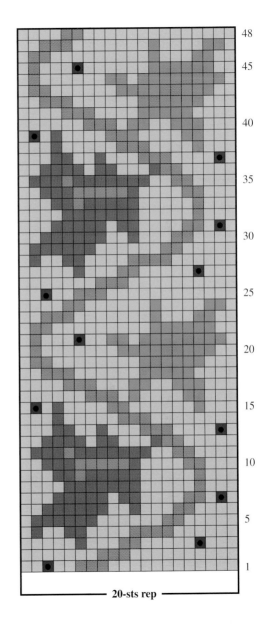

20-sts rep

For Intermediate Knitters

Colorful cotton socks move in the right circles. This retro box-and-circle print pattern, interpreted by Gitta Schrade, is updated in 90's brights.

SIZES

Instructions are for woman's size Medium. Changes for man's size Large are in parentheses.

MATERIALS

■ 2 .88oz/25g balls (each approx 69yd/62m) of Classic Elite *Cotton Sox* (cotton②) #4952 purple (MC)
■ 1 ball each of #4977 turquoise (A), #4958 red (B), #4935 lime (C), #4985 orange (D), #4996 yellow (E)
■ 1 set (4) each sizes 1 and 2 (2.25 and 2.5mm) double pointed needles (dpn) OR SIZE TO OBTAIN GAUGE
■ Stitch holder
■ Stitch markers
■ Tapestry needle

GAUGE

30 sts and 34 rnds to 4"/10cm over St st and chart pat using larger needles. TAKE TIME TO CHECK GAUGE.

Note When changing colors, twist yarns on WS to prevent holes.

CUFF

Beg at top edge with MC and one smaller needle, cast on 60 (72) sts. Divide sts onto three needles with 20 (24) sts on each needle. Join, taking care not to twist sts on needles. Mark end of rnds and sl marker every rnd. Working in k1, p1 rib with smaller needles, work 3 rnds MC; p 1 rnd with E, work 3 rnds in rib with E; p 1 rnd with D, work 3 rnds in rib with D; p 1 rnd with A, work 3 rnds in rib with A; p 1 rnd with B, work 3 rnds in rib with B; p 1 rnd with C, work 3 rnds in rib with C. Change to larger needles and work pat foll chart having 5 (6) 12-st reps. Work to row 35 of chart. Sock measures approx 4"/10cm in chart pat.

HEEL

Sl last 15 (18) sts from *Needle 3* and first 15 (18) sts from *Needle 1* onto one needle for heel—30 (36) sts for heel. Sl rem 30 (36) sts onto holder for instep. Work back and forth in rows on heel sts only. Cut yarn and reattach MC to heel sts and work in St st (k 1 row, p 1 row) for 16 (18) rows.

Turn heel
Next row K20 (24), SSK, turn.
Row 2 Sl 1, p10 (12), p2tog, turn.
Row 3 Sl 1, k10 (12), SSK, turn.
Rep last 2 rows until all sts are worked across—12 (14) heel sts rem.
Next rnd *Needle 3* with MC, k6 (7), pm for beg of rnd; *Needle 1* work chart rnd 1, sts 1-6 (1-7), cont in rnds and in chart pat, pick up and k 15 (17) sts from side of heel working chart sts 7-12 then 1-9 (8-12 then 1-12), pm for instep; *Needle 2* work 30 (36) instep sts from holder in chart sts 4-12, 1-12 then 1-9 (7-12, [1-12] twice, 1-6),

pm for instep; *Needle 3* pick up and k 15 (17) sts from side of heel in chart sts 4-12, then 1-6 (1-12, then 1-5), k rem sts from *Needle 3* in chart sts 7-12 (6-12).

Note Chart sts will not match until instep shaping is complete.

Shape instep

Rnd 1 K in chart pat as established until 2 sts before instep marker, k2tog, k to 2nd marker, SSK, k to end. Work 2 rnds even. Rep last 3 rnds until there are 60 (72) sts. Work even in pat until foot measures 7 (8¾)"/17.75 (22)cm or 2 (2¼)"/5 (5.75)cm less than desired length from back of heel to end of toe. End with 6th row of color box rep.

Shape toe

Divide sts so there are 15 (18) sts each on *Needle 1* and *Needle 3* and 30 (36) sts on *Needle 2*.

Rnd 1 With MC, *Needle 1* k to last 3 sts, k2tog, k1; *Needle 2* k1, SSK, k to last 3 sts, k2tog, k1; *Needle 3* k1, SSK, k to end. Work 3 rnds even. [Work rnd 1, work 2 rnds even] twice. [Work rnd 1, work 1 rnd even] 3 times. Then work rnd 1 only until 8 (12) sts rem. Divide sts on two needles and weave tog using Kitchener stitch.

Color key

■ Purple (MC)

□ Turquoise (A)

■ Red (B)

□ Lime (C)

▨ Orange (D)

□ Yellow (E)

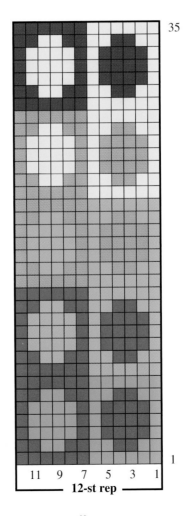

35

1

11   9   7   5   3   1

12-st rep

The splendid *adire* indigo-dyed cloths of the Yoruba people of Nigeria provided the inspiration for these graphic socks, designed by Jean Moss. The checkerboard pattern is the traditional foundation for many designs. Two-color cast-on creates an interesting cuff.

SIZES

Instructions are written for man's size Medium.

MATERIALS

■ 1 .80oz/25g hank (each approx 75yd/67m) of Rowan *Light Weight DK* (wool②) each in #603 cinnamon (MC), #80 chocolate (A), #655 mallard (B) and #77 rust (C)

■ 2 hanks each in #54 dark blue (D) and #6 vanilla (E)

■ 1 set (4) size 6 (4mm) double pointed needles (dpn) OR SIZE TO OBTAIN GAUGE

■ Stitch marker

GAUGE

24 sts and 28 rnds to 4"/10cm over St st and chart pat using size 6 (4mm) needles. TAKE TIME TO CHECK GAUGE.

Notes 1 When changing colors, twist yarns on WS to prevent holes.

2 Double cast-on method is used with two colors for cast-on edge of cuff. (see Basics section for technique)

STITCHES USED

Braid Pattern

Rnd 1 *K1 with C, k1 with A; rep from * around.

Rnd 2 Bring both colors to the front of the work. Keep them in the same order as on the previous rnd. *P1 with C, p1 with A, always bringing the next color to be used OVER the top of the last color used. Rep from * around.

Rnd 3 *P1 with C, p1 with A, always bringing the next color to be used UNDER the last color used. Rep from * around.

Rep rnds 1-3 for braid pat.

CUFF

Cast on 56 sts with C over the index finger, and A over the thumb, using the double cast-on method. Make a loop using both colors. (Loop does not figure in the total stitch count.) When all sts have been cast on, remove the loop made up of the two colors. Divide the sts evenly onto three needles. Join, taking care not to twist sts on needles. Mark end of rnd and sl marker every rnd. Work rnds 1-3 of braid pat twice, inc 1 st at beg and end of last rnd.

Next rnd Inc 1 st at beg and end of rnd, work rnd 1 foll chart—60 sts.

Cont to foll chart, working 10-st rep 6 times, through rnd 33. Then cont to work rnds 24-33 only (checkerboard pat), work 5 more rnds. Piece measures approx 6½"/16.5cm from beg. Cut yarns.

HEEL

Place the first 14 sts of the rnd and the last 15 sts onto *Needle 1* for heel. Divide the rem 31 sts onto *Needle 2* and *Needle 3* to be worked later for instep. Cont to work on 29 heel sts only, working back and forth with C and A as foll:

Row 1 (RS) *K1 with C, k1 with A; rep from *, end k1 with C, turn.

Row 2 *P1 with C, p1 with A; rep from *, end p1 with C, turn.

Rep these 2 rows for a total of 18 heel rows.

Turn heel

Next row (RS) [K1 with C, k1 with A] 9 times, k1 with C, k2tog tbl with A, turn.

Row 2 Sl 1 purlwise, [p1 with C, p1 with A] 4 times, p1 with C, p2tog with A, turn.

Row 3 Sl 1 purlwise, [k1 with C, k1 with A] 4 times, k1 with C, k2tog tbl with A, turn.

Rep last 2 rows until all sts are worked—11 sts, end with a WS row.

INSTEP

Gusset

Needle 1 work across 11 heel sts as foll: sl 1, k5 with D, k5 with E, then with E, pick up and k 14 sts along side of heel piece; *Needle 2* work across 31 instep sts cont in pat as before on instep, then pick up and k 1 st (for 32 sts on *Needle 2* or instep); *Needle 3* with E, pick up and k 13 sts along other side of heel piece, then sl first 6 sts from *Needle 1* onto end of *Needle 3*. There are 19 sts on *Needle 1*; 32 sts on *Needle 2*; and 19 sts on *Needle 3*—70 sts in total.

Shape gusset

Rnd 1 *Needle 1* k5 with E, k5 with D, k5 with E, k1 with D, k2tog with D, k1 with D; *Needle 2* SSK with D, k4 with D, [k5

with E, K5 with D] twice, k4 with E, k2tog with E; *Needle 3* k1 with E, SSK with E, k1 with E, k5 with D, k5 with E, k5 with D.

Rnd 2 Work in checkerboard pat as established.

Rnd 3 *Needle 1* k5 with E, k5 with D, k5 with E, k2tog with D, k1 with D; *Needle 2* [k5 with D, k5 with E] 3 times; *Needle 3* k1 with E, SSK with E, k5 with D, k5 with E, k5 with D.

Rnd 4 Rep rnd 2.

Cont to foll checkerboard pat in this way, working k2tog and k1 at end of *Needle 1*; work even on *Needle 2*; and k1, SSK at beg of *Needle 3*, every rnd twice more. There are 15 sts each on *Needle 1* and *Needle 3*, and 30 sts on *Needle 2*—a total of 60 sts. Work even in checkerboard pat until sock measures 8½"/21.5cm or 2½"/6.5cm less than desired length from back of heel to end of toe. (Make adjustments in length at this point.)

Shape toe

Rnd 1 Working with A only, work as foll: *Needle 1* k to last 3 sts, k2tog, k1; *Needle 2* k1, SSK, k to last 3 sts, k2tog, k1; *Needle 3* k1, SSK, k to end.

Rnd 2 With C, knit.

Rep last 2 rnds until there are 18 sts on *Needle 2*. Then cont in stripe pat, rep rnd 1 (dec rnd) only until there are 4 sts on *Needle 2*. Cut yarn . Draw through rem 8 sts and pull up to fasten. Secure and fasten off.

FINISHING

Block socks. Weave in ends neatly.

Color key

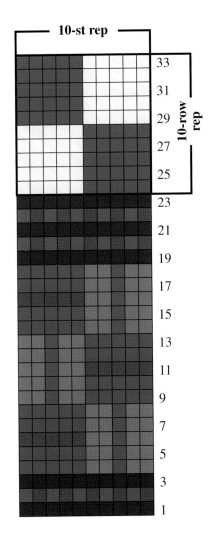

Cinnamon (MC)

Chocolate (A)

Mallard (B)

Rust (C)

Dark Blue (D)

Vanilla (E)

BED SOCKS

Garter stripes for cold winter nights

One-size-fits-all tube socks, designed by Jo Sharp, are worked in contrasting garter and stockinette stripes. Crocheted drawstrings keep them secure for toasty feet under the covers.

SIZE
One size fits all.

MATERIALS

Citrus Socks
- 2 1¾oz/50g balls (each approx 107yd/98m) of Jo Sharp *Supersoft Extra Fine DK* (wool③) in #509 citrus (MC)
- 1 ball in #502 olive brown (CC)

Mulberry Socks
- 2 1¾oz/50g balls (each approx 107yd/98m) of Jo Sharp *Supersoft Extra Fine DK* (wool③) in #501 mulberry (MC)
- 1 ball #323 beige (CC)

Both versions
- One pair size 6 (4mm) straight needles OR SIZE TO OBTAIN GAUGE
- One set (5) size 3 (3mm) double-pointed needles (dpn)
- Size E/4 (3.50mm) crochet hook
- Stitch markers

GAUGE
22 sts and 34 rows to 4"/10cm over St st using size 6 (4mm) needles. TAKE TIME TO CHECK GAUGE.

Note Cast on and work sock back and forth in rows on two needles to toe. Then join and work in rnds while shaping toe.

STITCHES USED

K1, P1 Rib
Row 1 (RS) *K1, p1; rep from * to end.
Row 2 (WS) K the knit sts and p the purl sts.
Rep row 2 for k1, p1 rib.

CUFF
Beg at top edge with size 6 (4mm) straight needles and MC, cast on 45 sts. Work in k1, p1 rib for 10 rows.
Row 11 (Eyelet row) K1, p1, k1, p2tog, yo, *p3, p2tog, yo*, work between *'s twice more, p1, p2tog, yo, p1, p2tog, yo, work between *'s 3 times, p1, k1, p1, k1—45 sts.
Row 12 P1, k1, p1, k1, p1, k to last 5 sts, p1, k1, p1, k1, p1.
Row 13 (RS) K1, p1, k1, p1, k1, p to last 5 sts, k1, p1, k1, p1, k1.
Row 14 Rep row 12.
Row 15 With MC rib 5 sts, with CC k to last 5 sts, with MC rib 5 sts.
Row 16 With MC rib 5 sts, with CC p to last 5 sts, with MC rib 5 sts.
Row 17 With MC rib 5 sts, k to last 5 sts, rib 5 sts.
Row 18 With MC rib 5 sts, k to last 5 sts, rib 5 sts.
Row 19 With MC rib 5 sts, p to last 5 sts, rib 5 sts.
Row 20 Rep row 18.
Rep rows 15-20 for pat 13 times more—piece measures approx 12"/30.5cm from beg. Adjust length of sock at this point if desired.

SHAPE TOE

With CC, k2tog then k 1 rnd dividing 11 sts on each of four needles—44 sts. Join, place marker for end of rnd and sl marker every rnd. Work around in St st (k every rnd) for 6 more rnds.

Rnd 8 [K8, k2tog, k2, k2tog, k8] twice.
Rnd 9 [K7, k2tog, k2, k2tog, k7] twice.
Rnd 10 [K6, k2tog, k2, k2tog, k6] twice.
Rnd 11 [K5, k2tog, k2, k2tog, k5] twice.
Rnd 12 [K4, k2tog, k2, k2tog, k4] twice.
Rnd 13 [K3, k2tog, k2, k2tog, k3] twice.
Rnd 14 [K2, k2tog, k2, k2tog, k2] twice.
Rnd 15 [K1, k2tog, k2, k2tog, k1] twice.

Rnd 16 [K2tog, k2, k2tog] twice—8 sts. Cut yarn leaving an end for sewing. Draw through sts on needle and fasten off.

FINISHING

Block lightly. With crochet hook and MC, working from RS, sl st front seam of sock tog.

Drawstring

With crochet hook and 1 strand each MC and CC held tog, make a chain 28"/70cm long. Knot ends and pull through eyelet row.

CORRUGATED SOCKS

Stylish stripes in space-dyes and solids

Multi-color variegated and solid-color striped socks designed by Victoria Mayo. Contrast garter stitch stripes create textural ridges of color.

SIZES

Instructions are for adult's size Small. Changes for sizes Medium and Large are in parentheses.

MATERIALS

■ 1 1¾oz/50g ball (each approx 176yd/162m) each of Koigu Wool Designs *Koigu Premium Merino* (wool③) in #2300 light blue (MC), #2120 fuchsia (B) and #2260 lilac (E)

■ 1 1¾oz/50g ball (each approx 176yd/162m) each of Koigu Wool Designs *Koigu Painter's Palette Premium Merino* (wool③) in #405 purple multi (A), #122 rainbow (C) and #116 green rainbow (D)

■ 1 set (4) size 4 (3.5mm) double pointed needles (dpn) OR SIZE TO OBTAIN GAUGE

■ Stitch markers

■ Tapestry needle

GAUGE

24 sts and 40 rnds to 4"/10cm over ridged stripe pat, stretched slightly, using size 4 (3.5mm) needles. TAKE TIME TO CHECK GAUGE.

CUFF

Beg at top edge with MC, cast on 52 sts on one needle. Divide sts onto three needles with 17 sts on *Needle 1*; 18 sts on *Needle 2*; and 17 sts on *Needle 3*. Join, taking care not to twist sts on needles. Mark end of rnd and sl marker every rnd.

Rnd 1 *K2, p2; rep from * around.
Rep rnd 1, for k2, p2 rib for 2"/5cm.

Beg ridged stripe pat *With A, p 5 rnds; with B, k 5 rnds; with C, p 5 rnds; with MC, k 5 rnds; with D, p 5 rnds; with E, k 5 rnds. Rep from * (30 rnds) for ridged stripe pat once more. Then with A, p 5 rnds. Piece measures approx 8½"/21.5cm from beg stretched lengthwise slightly.

HEEL

With MC, k13, sl next 26 sts onto two needles for instep, slide the last 13 sts onto end of *Needle 1* for heel. Work back and forth in rows on 26 heel sts only.

Row 1 (WS) Sl 1 purlwise, p to end.
Row 2 Sl 1, k to end.
Rep these 2 rows until heel measures 2¼"/5.75cm, end with row 2.

Turn heel
Next row (WS) P15 (half the number of sts plus 2), p2tog, p1, turn.
Row 2 Sl 1, k5, SSK, k1, turn.
Row 3 Sl 1, p6, p2tog, p1, turn.
Row 4 Sl 1, k7, SSK, k1, turn.
Cont in this way always having one more st before dec, and SSK on RS rows or p2tog on WS rows, until there are 16 sts on heel needle.

Instep

Sl last 8 sts of heel to spare needle, then cont to pick up and k (with same needle) 14 sts from side of heel, (22 sts on *Needle 1*); k26 sts of instep (*Needle 2*); pick up and k 14 sts from other side of heel and k last 8 sts (22 sts on *Needle 3*)—70 sts.

Shape instep

Rnd 1 K all sts.

Rnd 2 *Needle 1* k to last 3 sts, k2tog, k1; *Needle 2* knit; *Needle 3* k1, k2tog, k to end.

Rep these 2 rnds (cont in ridged stripe pat as before) until there are 52 sts on all three needles. Then work even in ridged stripe pat until foot measures 5½ (6½, 7½)"/ 14 (16.5, 19)cm (slightly stretched) or 2"/5cm less than desired length from back of heel to end of toe, end with 5 p rows.

Shape toe

Rnd 1 With MC, knit.

Rnd 2 With MC, *Needle 1* k to last 3 sts, k2tog, k1; *Needle 2* k1, SSK, k to last 3 sts, k2tog, k1; *Needle 3* k1, SSK, k to end. Rep these 2 rnds until 16 sts rem. Divide sts on two needles and weave tog using Kitchener stitch.

RESOURCES

US RESOURCES

Write to the yarn companies listed below for purchasing and mail-order information.

ALICE STARMORE
distributed by
The Broad Bay Co.

BERROCO, INC.
14 Elmdale Road
P.O. Box 367
Uxbridge, MA 01569

BROAD BAY CO.
P.O. Box 2935
Fort Bragg, CA 95437

BROWN SHEEP CO., INC.
100662 County Road 16
Mitchell, NE 69357

CLASSIC ELITE YARNS, INC.
12 Perkins Street
Lowell, MA 01854

CLECKHEATON
distributed by Plymouth Yarn

DALE OF NORWAY, INC.
N16 W23390 Stoneridge Drive
Suite A
Waukesha, WI 53188

GGH
distributed by Muench Yarns

JCA
35 Scales Lane
Townsend, MA 01469

JO SHARP
distributed by Classic Elite

KOIGU WOOL DESIGNS
R.R. #1
Williamsford, ON N0H 2V0
Canada

LANE BORGOSESIA
422 East Vermijo
Colorado Springs, CO 80903

LANG
distributed by Berroco, Inc.

LION BRAND YARNS
34 West 15th Street
New York, NY 10011
www.lionbrand.com

MUENCH YARNS
118 Ricardo Road
Mill Valley, CA 94941-2461

ORNAGHI FILATI
distributed by
Trendsetter Yarns

PLYMOUTH YARN
P.O. Box 28
Bristol, PA 19007

ROWAN
distributed by
Westminster Fibers

SCHOELLER-ESSLINGER
distributed by
Skacel Collection

SESIA
distributed by
Lane Borgosesia

SKACEL COLLECTION
P.O. Box 88110
Seattle, WA 98138-2110

STACY CHARLES COLLECTION
1059 Manhattan Avenue
Brooklyn, NY 11222

STAHL WOLLE
distributed by
Tahki Imports, Ltd.

TAHKI IMPORTS, LTD.
11 Graphic Place
Moonachie, NJ 07074

TRENDSETTER YARNS
16742 Stagg Street
Suite 104
Van Nuys, CA 91406

UNGER
distributed by JCA

WESTMINSTER FIBERS
5 Northern Boulevard
Amherst, NH 03031

CANADIAN RESOURCES

Write to US resources for mail-order availability of yarns not listed.

ALICE STARMORE
distributed by
Estelle Designs & Sales Ltd.

CLASSIC ELITE
distributed by
S. R. Kertzer Ltd

CLECKHEATON
distributed by Diamond Yarn

DIAMOND YARN
9697 St. Laurent
Montreal, PQ H3L 2N1 and
1450 Lodestar Road
Unit #4
Toronto, ON M3J 3C1

ESTELLE DESIGNS & SALES LTD.
Units 65/67
2220 Midland Avenue
Scarborough, ON M1P 3E6

FILATURA DI CROSA
distributed by Diamond Yarn

JO SHARP
distributed by Estelle Designs & Sales

S. R. KERTZER LTD.
105A Winges Road
Woodbridge, ON L4L 6C2

KOIGU WOOL DESIGNS
R.R. #1
Williamsford, ON N0H 2V0

LANG
distributed by R. Stein Yarn Corp.

STAHL WOLLE
distributed by Diamond Yarn

SCHOELLER-ESSLINGER
distributed by
S. R. Kertzer Ltd.

R. STEIN YARN CORP.
5800 St-Denis
Suite 303
Montreal, PQ H2S 3L5

ROWAN
distributed by
Diamond Yarn

UK RESOURCES

Not all yarns are available in the UK. For yarns not available, either make a comparable substitute or contact the US manufacturer for purchasing and mail-order information.

In the UK Cleckheaton is sold as Jarol Super Saver DK
JAROL LTD.
White Rose Mills
Cape Street
Canal Road
Bradford, BD1 4RN
Tel: 0274-392274

ROWAN YARNS
Green Lane Mill
Holmfirth
West Yorks HD7 1RW
Tel: 01484-681881

Alice Starmore Yarn is available from
SILKSTONE
12 Market Place
Cockermouth
Cumbria, CA13 9NQ
Tel: 01900-821052

VOGUE KNITTING SOCKS

Editor-in-Chief
TRISHA MALCOLM

Art Director, Butterick® Company, Inc
JOE VIOR

Book Designer
CHRISTINE LIPERT

Senior Editor
CARLA S. SCOTT

Managing Editor
DARYL BROWER

Associate Knitting Editor
TEVA MARGARET DURHAM

Technical Illustration Editor
LILA P. CHIN

Instructions Coordinator
CHARLOTTE PARRY

Yarn Coordinator
VERONICA MANNO

Instruction Writer
MARI LYNN PATRICK

Editorial Coordinators
KATHLEEN KELLY
ANNEMARIE McNAMARA

Photography
BRIAN KRAUS, NYC
Photographed at Butterick Studios

Project Directors
MARTHA MORAN
CAROLINE POLITI

Publishing Consultant
MIKE SHATZKIN, THE IDEALOGICAL COMPANY

■

President and Publisher, SOHO Publishing Company
ART JOINNIDES

Chairman, SOHO Publishing Company
JAY H. STEIN